GW00975951

Harrap's
New Outlook Series

Twentieth-Century
Stories of Action

Harrap's
New Outlook Series

TWENTIETH-CENTURY
STORIES OF ACTION

chosen and edited by

R. F. EGFORD, B.A.

and

A. J. WEEKS-PEARSON, B.A.

GEORGE G. HARRAP & CO. LTD
London · Toronto · Wellington · Sydney

First published in Great Britain 1969
as Life in Action
by GEORGE G. HARRAP & CO. LTD
182–184 High Holborn, London WC1V 7AX

ISBN 0 245 50908 9

Composed in Juliana type and printed by
Western Printing Services Ltd, Bristol
Made in Great Britain

ACKNOWLEDGMENTS

We should like to thank the following for permission to include stories in this collection:

MacGibbon and Kee, Ltd, for "The Key of the Cabinet" from *Late Night on Watling Street*, by Bill Naughton; Faber and Faber, Ltd, for "The Harvesting" from *Wodwo*, by Ted Hughes; Dr Mulk Raj Anand for "The Barber's Trade Union"; the Trustees for the copyrights of the late Dylan Thomas and J. M. Dent and Sons, Ltd, for "A Story" from *A Prospect of the Sea*; Mr Wolfgang Borchert and Penguin Books, Ltd, for "Thithyphuth", translated by Paul Dinnage, from *The Penguin Book of German Short Stories*; Edward Arnold (Publishers), Ltd, for "Casting the Runes" from *The Collected Short Stories of* M. R. *James*; Mr V. S. Naipaul and André Deutsch, Ltd, for "The Enemy" from *A Flag on the Island*; The Bodley Head for "The Burglars" from *The Golden Age*, by Kenneth Grahame; the Hogarth Press for "The Vertical Ladder" from *The Stories of William Sansom*; Jonathan Cape, Ltd, for "Fear" from *Thirty Tales*, by H. E. Bates.

Preface

MOST people expect something like 'blood and thunder', violent and sensational events, or at least physical action when they hear the term 'Action' applied to films or stories. Some of the stories in this book are about sensational or physically vigorous experience. Nevertheless, we hope to lead the reader on to recognize that the word action can apply to a much wider range of life experience. Linked with this idea is the fact that very often most is happening when it least appears to be.

R.F.E.
A.J.W-P.

Contents

The Key of the Cabinet

BILL NAUGHTON

"NOW here you are," said my mother, putting the coins down on the edge of the dresser, "your Friday four-pence."

"Could I have my Saturday sixpence at the same time, Mam?" I said. "It 'ud save you the trouble tomorrow."

"It'll be no trouble," she said, "if I have it to give. Off you go."

I went to the door and out into the street. There was something gloomy about February, even on a Friday. Christmas was well behind you, marble and top-and-whip season not in yet. I set off for Ma Enty's shop to buy some everlasting toffee.

I was halfway down the street when suddenly I heard a loud bang from the street corner. I went running up to see what it was when I saw my mate, Ernie Egan.

"Wut was that, Ernie?"

"Ned Anderson striking off a key."

"Gerroff," I said. "'Strike the key' season hasn't started."

"Go an' see," said Ernie. "It's just broke out all over the place. Lads are goin' mad. I'm off to find m'own key."

I ran to the street corner as three more bangs sounded. I saw half a dozen of my mates on the swing and others loading up. Each one had a key, a hollow key, fastened to a length of string, with a long nail tied to the other end. I went and stood beside Ned Anderson, who was just loading up.

"How do, Ned?" I said.

He lifted his head and gave a brief nod. I watched as his

9

fingers carefully loaded the hollow barrel of the key with a mixture of brimstone and potash. Then with a matchstick he made the charge firm before inserting the nail into the barrel, and then he delicately blew away the surplus powder. The nail was now nicely embedded in the key, with about two inches and a good head of it free. Ned held the string in the middle, like you might hold the handle of a basket, with the key and nail dangling. Then he fixed his eye on a nice hard smooth brick on the gable-end, and he began to swing the string to and fro, until eye and hand were in, and then he sent it swinging through the air, so that the head of the nail struck the wall clean and hard. There was a loud bang, and the fumes got in my eyes.

"Good lad, Ned," I cried out. "That was a right good bang. It was a real beauty, Ned. Wut about me havin' a go?"

"Wut—with my key? Let you have a go with my key an' powder?" He stared at me as though he couldn't believe his own ears. "Wut d'you think I've just come off—an onion boat?"

I quickly went round amongst the others, but I couldn't catch a single eye, and I knew at once there was only one thing for it: I had to go off and find my own key. I knew where there was one from last year in an old drawer. I got it and a nail and some string. Then I went off to Daddy Clough's chemist's shop and bought two pennyworth of ready-mixed brimstone and potash.

I was soon back at the street corner swinging my own key-and-nail, and swinging pretty well at that. I was getting one good bang-off in three, and bringing out complaining neighbours. Of course, what I was actually going all out for was the loudest bang, and as my eye was getting in I was fairly breathless with pleasure. The next thing, I noticed Ernie Egan beside me.

"Wut's up, Ernie?" I said.

"Cannot lay m'hands on a key, Bill, not for love nor brass," said Ernie.

10

"Hard cheddar," I said, loading up again.

"Ee, that was a right good bang, Bill," said Ernie. "A right beauty. Uh, Bill, wut about me havin' a go?"

"Wut—wi' my key?" I said. "Thee have a go wi' my key! Hold your hush, Ernie—wut d'you think I've come off, a banana boat?"

He said no more but just watched. I thought it was a bit thick his asking. It was like asking a chap who was fishing could you hold his rod-and-line when his float was under. But Ernie had a *way* of looking. Suddenly I turned on him.

"One go an' no more!" I said. "An' listen, if tha dares to bend that nail, Ernie Egan, I'll take it out of thy ribs twice over."

"Agreed, agreed," said Ernie. "Listen, if I so much as bring that nail one thou' of an inch out of line, I'll kneel me down there on that sideset, an' you can par me with all your might with your clog-toe. On my scout's honour. Now let me load it."

"Load it? Some hopes you've got! D'you think I'm going to let you load *my* key? I'm not *that* green, even though I am cabbage-looking. I'll load, you'll fire, an' be sharp about it."

'Course, half the job of firing a thing is loading it up yourself, and poor Ernie didn't have his eye in either, so that his aim was bog-eyed, and he sent it too hard, and the strike went skew-whiff, and there was no explosion.

"Hand over," I said, "let the dog see the rabbit."

I pulled the nail out and held it before Ernie's nose.

"See wut you've done!"

Ernie nodded, and with a sigh of resignation knelt on the pavement and exhibited his britches seat to me. "Try not to rip 'em if tha can," he said.

For a moment I looked down on the kneeling figure. Ernie was too bony to be tempting. When I touched him on the shoulder he nearly jumped in the air.

"Get up, Ernie," I said. "There's not much in this for either

11

of us." He didn't contradict me. "Now, Ernie, instead of sufferin' the penalty, suppose you went home an' pinched a nail for me?"

"Aye, I suppose I could," said Ernie. "But if my dad catches me in his nail-box he'll not give me an alternative to his clog-toe. An' his happens to be about seven times the size of yours."

"Then don't let him catch thee!"

Ernie slouched off. That's the last I'll see of him tonight, I thought. But I was wrong. Five minutes later I saw Egan's door open, and out came Ernie on tiptoe. He crept softly past their window-sill, his head ducked, and suddenly he gave a leap and let out a great whoop of joy.

"Got it?" I cried, pouncing on him.

He opened his fist. Lying there in the palm of his hand was a thick silvery key.

"Oo, wut a beaut!" I picked it up and examined it. It was very heavy, with a large smooth barrel. "Ah, but there's one thing you've forgotten, Ernie, you'll never in this world get a nail to fit that key."

Ernie smiled and dipped down into his pocket and produced two nails: one a fat shiny nail and the other a long nail. "Take the long 'un, Bill, it's thine. The fat 'un's mine. It's a perfect fit. But listen, dunna let a soul hear about this key!"

"For why, Ernie?"

"It's off my dad's Chippendale Chinese cabinet."

"Wut, that old glass-fronted thing wi' the velvet box inside?"

"*Sh, sh!* He'd go clean off his rocker if he knew."

"But won't he see it's gone?"

Ernie shook his head, "He keeps the key hid away. That's how I found it—hid in a little tin amongst all the nails. An' he only opens it of a weekend through the winter."

"How come, Ernie?"

"He keeps his chrono' inside that velvet box," said Ernie.

12

"That's his stop-watch for timin' his pigeons. He'll need it tomorrow."

"Then wut the flappin' Nora are you worritin' about, lad?" I said. "You can put it back when you've done."

Ernie looked upwards: "Ooh, if only he found out!" and he gave a shiver.

"Want some loadin' powder, Ernie?"

"No, I'll buy m'own," he said. "An' I'll mix it myself."

He was soon back, with two separate packets: one of brimstone and the other potash. With his head hidden under his jacket he began to load the silver key. When it was ready I watched as he took his strike. He swung it gingerly and got no bang. Then he tried again and again, and every time he failed. He used new mixtures, but it was no use. The glamour went from the key.

"Ernie, you'll never get a bang out of that in the memory of man," I said.

"I'm goin' to put an extra heavy loadin' of potash in this time," said Ernie, after his tenth miss.

A quiet lad when he was quiet, Ernie had a bit of a demon in him when he got worked up. And I watched him, for I could see he was getting worked up. He wedged a mighty load inside the key, "You'll bang this time," he said, "or I'll know why."

I put down my own key and watched Ernie. He got on his toes and began to spin round like a ballet dancer. When he had got a good speed up, the string whizzing through the air, he struck the nail-head hard and square against the wall. For a moment nothing seemed to happen. Missed again, I thought, when suddenly I saw a flash. The next instant there was an explosion that shut off all sound. It seemed like my two ears had got all waxed up at once. Everything about went still and silent. Through a haze of blue smoke I could see Ernie—standing flabbergast with joy.

Then doors shot open all over the street, and dogs barked, and all the lads came running round.

13

"Wut the heck were that?"

"Who were it?"

"Wut a bang!"

"Look, he's blown half a brick outa the wall!"

"Wut mixture were it, Ernie?"

Ernie was like a lad in a dream. The biggest bang of the night. I led him away to recover. And then I spotted the dangling key.

"Don't look this very second, Ernie," I said, "but when tha has a minute to spare have a look at thy key."

Ernie looked down at the key. He couldn't speak. The silver key of Ernie's dad's Chippendale Chinese cabinet was ripped open right up the middle! That explosion had torn it in two like a bit of old newspaper.

"Stop! don't touch it, Ernie," I cried. "It's red hot."

"Oh . . . ooh! if my dad finds out!" said Ernie. "He'll lay me out."

"Aye," I said, "but it was a brawmin' good bang."

"Aye, it was a good 'un," said Ernie, smiling.

Just then a door opened down the street and we heard a woman calling, "Ernie! Ernie! you're wanted."

He grabbed my sleeve, "Don't leave me, Bill!"

"Duck thy head between thy knees, Ernie," I said, "an' fetch a bit of colour to thy face. Wrap that key up in thy hanky an' stuff it into thy pocket."

"Put it in thine," he said.

Ernie's father was waiting for us. A glassblower, big and hefty, sticking-out lips, red eyes and a voice like a factory buzzer.

"Has tha seen the key?" he asked.

"Wut key, Dad?" said Ernie. "I've just been to the library with Bill."

"Tha knows wut key," said Ernie's father.

Ooh, what a rasp of a voice that man had!

"Ee, no, Dad, I aren't seen that," said Ernie.

He dragged me into the house with him. His father went

14

over to the cabinet and began to tug at it as though he'd wrench the door off.

"You'll find it tomorrow, Dad," said Ernie's mother. "You've just mislaid it."

"I want it tonight," roared the man.

I don't know what he might have done if there hadn't been a call at the door, "Ready, Ezra?"

He looked at his wife, "If that key's not laid on that table when I get back——" he whispered, and then he went off.

Ernie's mother let her legs bend slowly until she was resting on the edge of a chair. Ernie's look of fear went.

"I'm sorry, Mum," he said.

"Not your fault, love," she said.

"Oh yes it is, Mam," said Ernie. "I took the key."

"Ee, I thought it was God had done it," she said. She pulled him over by his jersey, and rubbed his head at the back, "You've saved my life, love."

Ernie looked mystified. "I thought he were goin' to hit you, Mam," he said.

"He woulda done if he'd ha' opened it," she said. "His watch isn't there."

"Where is it, Mum?"

"There are times, luv," she said, "when folk get short of money midweek. Then they gotta have summat to borrow a bit with." She suddenly got up and grabbed her shawl and went off.

"Where's she gone, Ernie?"

"Pop shop," said Ernie. "Gettin' his chrono' out. She didn't expect he'd look for it till tomorrow. Good job I bust that key."

"But how is she going to get the watch back inside?" I asked.

"Oo, crumbs! Let's have a look at that key," said Ernie. I took the hanky from my pocket and took out the key.

"If only we could file the ripped part off, Ernie, an' press t'other part in a vice, we might open it."

We locked the front door and went to work on it. And with some tape we were able to open the cabinet, just as Ernie's mother got back. But when we pulled the key out it fell apart, in two pieces.

"How did you do that, luv?" asked his mother.

"Didn't you hear that bang, Mum?" said Ernie. "It were me."

"Let me get this perishin' second-jumper back," said Ernie's mother. She put it carefully away inside the velvet box. Then she closed the glass doors.

"Wut shall we do, Mum?" asked Ernie.

"Say naught about it, lads. Here, Billy," she said to me, "take this key and fling it as far as you can into Taylor's mill lodge. Wait till you hear it splash."

When I got back Ernie said, "Did you do it?"

"Sir King, behold an arm clothed in white samite, mystic wonderful——" I said.

"Did tha fling it?"

"Aye, an' killed a couple of tiddlers."

"Go for some chips an' peas, luv," said his mother.

Ernie kept me there. Then in the distance we heard a heavy *clack-clack* of clogs. I looked to the door but Ernie held on. "Happen it won't be as bad if you're here," he said.

When Ezra Egan clomped in the front door he took no more notice of me than an old cap. He looked at his wife, "Have you found it?" he said.

"I'm sorry," she said, "I haven't."

"Right," he said, "I'll show you."

He went across to the cabinet, stood in front of it, drew back his right foot, and with one kick sent his clog-toe right through the glass front. And as the tinkling din of smashed glass died away he put his hand in and grabbed the velvet box. He went to the table and put it down. Then he looked at Ernie's mother.

"Now we'll see why that key were missin'!" he said.

We watched as he opened the box. His face went pale as he

saw the chronometer. He looked at the silver instrument and he thumped his forehead with his big fist.

"Mother, I've wronged you," he said.

I got up and slipped off, for this time Ernie didn't need to hold me back.

The Harvesting

TED HUGHES

---

*"And I shall go into a hare
with sorrow and sighs and mickle care."*

MR GROOBY kept his eyes down. The tractor and reaper below, negotiating the bottom right corner of the narrow, steep triangle of wheat, bumbled and nagged and stopped and started. The sweat trickled at the corner of his eye. Not a breath of air moved to relieve him. A dull atmosphere of pain had settled just above eye-level, and he had the impression that the whole top of heaven had begun to glare and flame.

For nearly three hours, since nine that morning, not the faintest gossamer of cloud had intervened between the sun and the thin felt of his trilby. A sunbather would have escaped to cover an hour ago.

Ten more minutes would finish the field. The best sport of all, he knew, usually comes in the last ten minutes. He would be a fool to go off and miss that after waiting for it, earning it, so to speak, all morning.

Laying his gun over a prone sheaf, he stripped off his waistcoat and draped that beside the gun, then raised his trilby and mopped the bald dome under it with his handkerchief, taking a few steps out and back again to bring the air to some coolness against his brow.

This was surely unnatural heat. He could remember nothing like it. The hanging dust raised by the tractor and the hurrying blade of the cutter absorbed the sun's vibrations till

18

it seemed hot as only a solid substance ought to be. And the spluttering reports, the dense machine-gun bursts from the tractor as it started up the gradient, tore holes in the blanketing air with something even fierier and deadlier. Near the edge of the field the dark, scorched-looking figures of out-of-work or off-work colliers, gathering the sheafs into stooks, with their black or tan whippets bounding around them, and one big, white, bony greyhound, appeared hellish, as if they flitted to and fro in not quite visible flames.

This was Grooby's first day out in the open since the previous summer. He had intended to stay out for only a couple of hours, expecting the field to be finished by eleven. Two hours today, four or five tomorrow, and so on, acclimatizing himself gradually, till he could take a whole day and enjoy the whole harvest. Perhaps three hours was a bit too much to begin with; perhaps he was overdoing it.

Ten more minutes then, and he would have to leave. Ten more minutes and after that, no matter how little of the field was left to cut, he would leave. He didn't want to spoil his holiday at the start.

By standing perfectly still, leaving his body to the sun's rays and shrinking inwardly from all its surfaces, he found he could defy both the slowness of time and the huge enveloping weight of the heat. He crouched in a tiny darkness somewhere near the bottom of his spine and dreamed of his car in the stone barn half a mile behind him across the fields. He smelt the cool leather of the upholstery and the fresh, thickly-daubed mustard and beef sandwiches lying there with two bottles of beer under the rug of the back seat.

The tractor came up to make its looping turn at the top corner. As Grooby stepped back, the grizzled chimpanzee figure at the wheel shouted something to him and jabbed a finger down toward the wheat, and the long dark-brown creature perched above the cutter shouted, and pointed at the wheat, while the shuddering combination slewed round on itself, suddenly disgorging its roar over Grooby as if a door had opened. Then the blade swept in again, wheat ears raining down under the red paddles of the reaper, every few feet a new sheaf leaping out on to the stubble—so many activities, so much hot busy iron, in a wake of red dust, drawing off, leaving Grooby isolated and surprisingly whole, as if he too had been tossed out like one of the sheafs.

Roused, he stepped up close and resumed his watch down the two diverging walls of stalks. The shouts of the farmer and his man meant they had seen something in the patch. Whatever remained in there would be whisking from side to side like a fish trapped in shallowing water as the reaper closed in. Grooby held his gun in the crook of his left arm, like a baby, fondling the chased side-plates and trigger-guard and mentally rehearsing for the hundredth time the easy swing, overtaking the running shape with a smooth squeeze on the trigger and follow through—one gliding, effortless motion, like a gesture in conversation.

Fifty yards behind him, two dead rabbits lay under a sheaf. He had missed three. His shooting was not good. But he loved the occasion—or rather, he had looked forward to it, remembering the days last summer when rabbits had been flying out in all directions, getting themselves snagged in the cutter, or bowled over by the colliers' sticks, or rolled in a flurry of dust by the dogs, and he himself shooting to left and right like a hero at a last stand. That was the sport, banging away.

But last summer there had been no such heat. He wondered if the farmer thought it unusual. Maybe it was a record heat-wave following the freakish dispersal during the night of some protective layer in the upper atmosphere. The Sunday papers would be full of it, with charts and historical comparisons.

Or maybe he was simply growing old, beginning to fail in the trials. He imagined there must be certain little tests that showed the process clearly: a day of rain, the first snow or, as now, a few hours of sun. Were these to become terrors? And he had put on a few pounds since last summer.

The trilby was a mistake. His brain felt black and numb and solid, like a hot stone. Tomorrow he would bring a broad-brimmed Panama hat. The stookers would snigger, no doubt, but they knotted handkerchiefs over their heads, like little boys.

He watched the tractor turning again at the bottom of the strip and it was now, as the tractor started up the slope towards him, that a strange sensation came over Grooby. Whether at the idea of all the energy needed and being exerted to drag such weight of vibrating iron up that hill in that heat, or at the realization that here was help approaching, and he could therefore allow himself to yield a little to the sun, he suddenly lost control of his limbs and felt himself floating in air a few feet above the crushed stubble.

He sat down hastily, adjusting his pose to look as natural as possible, but nevertheless alarmed and with a deep conviction that he was too late. He had closed his eyes and heard a voice in the darkness announcing over and over, in a brisk, businesslike tone, that he would now leave the field immediately. The sun had gathered to a small red spot in the top of his brain. He thought with terror of the distance back to the farm and safety: the short walk seemed to writhe and twist like a filament over a gulf of fire.

Opening his eyes, he found the tractor's Ford headplate, as it climbed towards him, centring his vision, and like a drunken man he anchored his attention to that as if it were the last spark of consciousness. Slowly his head cleared. He changed his position.

And now, as the world reassembled, he became aware that the farmer was standing erect in the tractor, waving his free arm and shouting. Grooby looked round for some explanation. The stookers had stopped work and were looking towards him almost like leashed dogs, while the dogs themselves craned round, quivering with anxiety, tucking their tails in for shame at seeing nothing where they knew there was something, eager to see something and be off. Grooby took all this

21

in remotely, as through the grill of a visor. He had a dim notion that they were all warning him back from the brink of something terrible. Then his eyes focused.

A yard out from the wall of wheat, ten yards from Grooby and directly in the path of the tractor, a large hare sat erect.

It stared fixedly, as if it had noted some suspicious detail in the far distance. Actually it was stupefied by this sudden revelation of surrounding enemies. Driven all morning from one side of the shrinking wheat to the other, terrified and exhausted by the repeated roaring charge and nearer and nearer miss of the tractor in its revolutions, the hare's nerves had finally cracked and here it was in the open, trying to recognize the strangely shorn hillside, confronted by the shapes of men and dogs, with the tractor coming up again to the left and a man scrambling to his feet on the skyline above to the right.

So it sat up, completely nonplussed.

Grooby aimed mercilessly. But then he perceived that the farmer's shouts had redoubled and altered in tone, and the farmhand on the cutter had joined in the shouting, flourishing his arms, with violent pushing movements away to his left, as if Grooby's gun muzzles were advancing on his very chest. Accordingly, Grooby realized that the tractor, too, lay above his gun barrels. He held his aim for a moment, not wanting to forgo his prior claim on the hare, and glanced over towards the dogs, flustered and angry. But for those dogs the hare would surely have run straight out, giving a clean, handsome shot. Now, any moment, the dogs would come clowning across the field, turn the hare back into the wheat and hunt it right through and away out at the bottom into the uncut field of rye down there, or round the back of the hill into the other fields.

To anticipate the dogs, Grooby started to run to the left, down the other side of the wheat, thinking to bring the hare against open background. But before he had gone three strides, the hare was off, an uncertain, high-eared, lolloping gait, still unable to decide the safe course or the right speed, till the dogs came ripping long smouldering tracks up the field and Grooby fired.

He forgot all about swing and squeeze and follow through. He was enraged, off balance, distracted by the speeding dogs and at all times hated shots from left to right. But his target loomed huge, close and moving slowly. The gun jarred back on his shoulder. The hare somersaulted, as if tossed into the air by the hind legs, came down in a flash of dust and streaked back into the wheat.

For a second, Grooby thought he must have fainted. He could hear the farmer yelling to the colliers to call their dogs off, threatening to shoot the bloody lot, but the voice came weirdly magnified and distorted as if his hearing had lost its muting defences. His head spun in darkness. He knew he had fallen. He could hear the tractor protesting on the gradient and it seemed so near, the engine drove so cruelly into his ears, he wondered if he had fallen in front of it. The ground trembled beneath him. Surely they would see him lying there! His senses cleared a little and as at the moment of waking from nightmare to the pillow and the familiar room, Grooby realized he was lying face downward in the wheat.

He must have fainted and staggered into the wheat and fallen there. But why hadn't they noticed him? Twisting his head, he saw what he could scarcely believe, the red, paddling flails of the reaper coming up over him. Within seconds those terrible hidden ground-shaving blades would melt the stalks and touch him—he would be sawn clean in two. He had seen them slice rabbits like bacon.

He uttered a cry, to whoever might hear, and rolled sideways, dragging himself on his elbows, tearing up the wheat in his hands as he clawed his way out of the path of the mutilator, and cried again, this time in surprise, as a broad wrench of pain seemed to twist off the lower half of his body, so that for a moment he thought the blades had caught him. With a final convulsion he threw himself forward and sprawled parallel to the course of the tractor.

LIFE IN ACTION

This is how it happens, his brain was yammering: it can happen, it can happen, and it's happened. This is how it happens. Everything is going nicely, then one careless touch, one wink of distraction, and your whole body's in the mincer, and you're in the middle of it, the worst that can happen forever. You've never dreamed it possible and all your life it's been this fraction of a second away, a hair's breadth from you, and here it is, here it is.

The noise of the tractor and the special grinding clatter of the cutter seemed to come up out of the raw soil taking possession of all the separate atoms of his body. The tractor's outline rose black against the blue sky and Grooby saw the farmer standing at the wheel, looking down. He cried out and waved an arm, like a drowning man, whereupon the farmer pointed at him, shouting something. Then the flails came over, and he heard the blades wuthering in the air. For a second everything disintegrated in din, chaffy fragments and dust, then they had gone past, and Grooby lay panting. Why hadn't they stopped? They saw him and went straight past. The end of the cutter bar had gone by inches from his face, and now he could see through the thin veil of stalks and out over the naked stubble slope. Why hadn't they stopped and got down to help him? He gathered himself and once more tried to get to his feet, but the baked clods of soil and the bright, metallic stalks of wheat fled into a remote silent picture as the pain swept up his back again and engulfed him.

But only for a moment. He jerked up his head. Hands held his shoulders, and someone splashed his face with water that ran down his neck and over his chest. He shook himself free and stood. As if he had tripped only accidentally, he began to beat the dust from his trousers and elbows, ignoring the ring of men who had come up and stood in a circle watching. All the time he was trying to recall exactly what happened. He remembered, as if touching a forgotten dream, that he had been lying in the wheat. Had they carried him out then? He flexed his back cautiously, but that felt easy, with no trace of discomfort. The farmer handed him his trilby. "All right now?"

He nodded. "Gun must have caught me off balance. Only explanation. Held it too loose. Knocked me clean out."

He adopted his brusquest managerial air, putting the farmer and this gang of impudent, anonymous colliers' faces back into place. What had they seen, he wondered. They could tell him. But how could he possibly ask?

"One of those flukes," he added.

The farmer was watching him thoughtfully, as if expecting him to fall again.

"Well, what happened to the hare?" Grooby demanded.

His continued gusty assurance took effect. Whatever they had seen or were suspecting, they had to take account of this voice. The farmer nodded, in his ancient, withered-up way.

"You're all right, then." He turned on the stookers in surprising fury. "*What the hell am I paying you for?*"

As they all trooped off down the field with their sullen dogs, the farmer started the tractor up and the cutter blade blurred into life.

Left alone, Grooby sank into a shocked stupor. His mind whirled around like a fly that dared not alight. A black vacancy held him. Something important was going on, if only he could grasp it. He seemed unable to move, even to wipe away the sweat that collected in his eyebrows and leaked down into his eyes. It occurred to him that the sun had settled over the earth, so that the air was actually burning gas, depth of flame in every direction. He watched the tractor dwindle in the bottom of the field, as if it were melting into a glittering puddle in the haze. How could men go on working in that temperature? The stookers were clearly charring; they were black as burnt twigs, tiny black ant men moving on the grey field.

One cut up and one down would finish the piece, and this prospect partly revived Grooby, including him once more in events. As the tractor waded up one side—now only fifteen yards or so long—he walked down the other, scrutinizing the thin curtain of stalks where every clump of wheat had ears and seemed to be sitting up alert.

At the bottom, a few paces back into the stubble, Grooby took up his position for the final sweep. Now the hare must either show itself or be killed by the cutter, unless it had already died in there of that first shot. As the tractor bore down, the colliers left their work, edging forward till Grooby noticed they had moved up level with him, as if to supervise the kill. He advanced a little, separating himself. The thought that the hare's first appearance would bring two or three dogs dancing across the line of fire unnerved him. Also, he didn't want these men to be looking at his face, which felt to be ludicrously pink and sweating its very fat.

If only the tractor would hurry up and get it over with or if only the hare would gather its wits and move. But the tractor seemed to have stopped. Grooby blinked and straightened himself vigorously, and that brought the tractor on a little more quickly. From the lowest corner of the wheat the few stalks that would be last to fall leaned out and tormented him in those endless seconds.

Then all at once here was the hare, huge as if nothing else existed. The colliers shouted, and the gun jumped to Grooby's shoulder. But he held his fire. The animal was too near. He saw the roughness of its brindled, gingery flanks and the delicate lines of its thin face. Besides, it seemed to want to surrender, and was so obviously bewildered that for a moment Grooby felt more like shooing it away to safety than shooting it dead. But it had already realized its folly and swerving sharply to Grooby's right, launched itself up the hill like a dart, a foot above the ground, while the farmer stood shouting in the tractor as those last stalks fell and the dogs behind Grooby climbed the air, yelling and coughing on their restraining collars.

He had bare seconds, he knew, before the dogs broke loose all around him, and it was with half his attention behind him that Grooby fired, at ten yards' range. The hare flattened in a scatter of dust, but was on its feet again, flogging its way up the slope, more heavily now, its hind-quarters collapsing every few strides. It looked just about finished, and rather than spoil it with the choke barrel or miss it clean, and also in order to be ahead of those dogs whatever happened, Grooby set off at a lumbering run. Immediately the hare picked up and stretched away ahead. Grooby stopped and aimed. The sweat flooded his eyes and he felt he ought to sit. He heard the shouting, and wiping his eyes and brow with one fierce movement along his left arm, brought his cheek back to the gun as one of the whippets ripped past him like a lit trail of gunpowder. He aimed furiously towards the bounding shape of the hare and fired.

The blackness struck him. The wild realization that he had done it again, the blasted gun had hit him again, was swallowed up.

He seemed to have fallen forward and thought he must have gone head over heels. One need possessed him. It drove him to struggle up the hill. None of his limbs belonged to him any more, and he wondered if he still lay in the wheat and whether the cutter blades had indeed gone over him. But loudest of all he heard the dogs. The dogs were behind him with their inane yapping. He began to shout at them and shouted louder than ever when he heard the sound that twisted from his throat, the unearthly thin scream. Then the enormous white dog's head opened beside him, and he felt as if he had been picked up and flung, and lost awareness of everything save the vague, pummelling sensations far off in the blankness and silence of his body.

The Barber's Trade Union

MULK RAJ ANAND

AMONG the makers of modern India, Chandu, the barber boy of our village, has a place which will be denied him unless I press for the recognition of his contribution to history. Chandu's peculiar claim to recognition rested, to tell the truth, on an exploit of which he did not know the full significance. But then, unlike most great men of India today, he had no very exaggerated notion of his own importance, though he shared with them a certain naïve egotism which was sometimes disconcerting and sometimes rather charming.

I knew Chandu ever since the days when he wore a piece of rag in the middle of his naked, distended-bellied body, and when we wallowed together in the mire of the village lanes, playing at soldiering, shopkeeping, or clerking, and other little games which we invented for the delectation of our two selves and of our mothers, who alone of all the elders condescended to notice us.

Chandu was my senior by about six months, and he always took the lead in all matters. And I willingly followed, because truly he was a genius at catching wasps, and at pressing the poison out of their tails, at tying their tiny legs to cotton and flying them, while I always got stung on the cheeks if I dared to go anywhere near the platform of the village well where these insects settled on the puddles to drink water.

When we grew up he still seemed to me the embodiment of perfection, because he could make and fly paper kites of such intricate design and of such balance as I could never achieve.

To be sure, he was not so good at doing sums at school as I

28

was, perhaps because his father apprenticed him early to the hereditary profession of the barber's caste and sent him out hair-cutting in the village, and he had no time for the home tasks which our schoolmaster gave us. But he was better than I at reciting poetry, any day, for not only did he remember by rote the verses in the text-book, but he could repeat the endless pages of prose in that book so that they seemed like poetry.

My mother resented the fact that Chandu won a scholarship at school while I had to pay fees to be taught. And she constantly dissuaded me from playing with him, saying that Chandu was a low-caste barber's son and that I ought to keep up the status of my caste and class. But whatever innate ideas I had inherited from my forefathers, I certainly hadn't inherited any sense of superiority. Indeed, I was always rather ashamed of the red caste mark which my mother put on my forehead every morning, and of the formalized pattern of the *uchkin*, the tight cotton trousers, the gold-worked shoes and the silk turban in which I dressed; and I longed for the right to wear all the spectacular conglomeration of clothes which Chandu wore—a pair of khaki shorts which the retired Subedar had given him, a frayed black velvet waistcoat, decorated all over with shell buttons, and a round felt cap which had once belonged to Lalla Hukam Chand, the lawyer of our village.

And I envied Chandu the freedom of movement which he enjoyed after his father died of plague. For then he would do the round of shaving and hair-cutting at the houses of the high-caste notables in the morning, bathe and dress, and then steal a ride to town, six miles away, on the foot-rest of the closed carriage in which Lalla Hukam Chand travelled to town.

But Chandu was kind to me. He knew that I was seldom taken to town, and that I had to trudge three weary miles to a secondary school in the big village of Joadiala with the fear of God in my heart, while he had been completely absolved from

29

the ordeal of being flogged by cruel masters as he had left school after his father's death. So he always brought me some gift or other from the town—a paint brush, or gold ink, or white chalk, or a double-edged penknife to sharpen pencils with; and he would entertain me with long merry descriptions of the variety of things he saw in the bazaars of civilization.

He was particularly detailed in his description of the wonderful English styles in clothes which he saw the Sahibs and the lawyers, the chaprasis, and the policemen wearing at the District Court, where he had to wait for the journey home at the back of Lalla Hukam Chand's phaeton. And, once or twice, he expressed to me a secret wish he had to steal some money from the pitcher where his mother kept the emoluments of his professional skill, to buy himself a rig-out like that of Kalan Khan, the dentist, who, he said, performed miracles in the town, fitting people with rows of teeth and even new eyes. He described to me the appearance of Kalan Khan, a young man with hair parted on one side, and dressed in a starched shirt, with an ivory collar and bow tie, a black coat and striped trousers, and a wonderful rubber overcoat and pumps. And he recounted to me the skill with which this magician unpacked an Angrezi leather handbag and flourished his shining steel instruments.

Then he asked my advice on the question of whether, as a barber educated to the fifth primary class, he would not look more dignified if he, too, wore a dress in the style of Dr Kalan Khan, "for though I am not a highly-educated doctor," he said, "I learnt how to treat pimples, boils and cuts on peoples' bodies from my father, who learnt them from his father before him."

I agreed with his project and encouraged him with the enthusiasm I felt for everything that my hero thought or did.

One day I was thrilled to find Chandu at the door of my house in the morning. He was dressed up in a white turban, a white rubber coat (a little too big for him, but nevertheless very splendid), a pair of pumps in which I could see my face reflected in clear silhouette, and he had a leather bag in his hand. He was setting off on his round and he had come to show me how grand he looked in his new rig-out.

"Marvellous!" I said. "Marvellous!"

And he rushed off towards the house of the landlord, whom he shaved every morning, myself following admiringly behind.

There were not many people in the street at this time. So I alone witnessed the glory of Chandu, dressed up as a doctor, except, of course, that he himself seemed rather self-conscious as he strutted up the street, carefully avoiding the taint of cow-dung cakes which the village women stuck to the walls, and the dirty water which flowed through the drains. But as we entered the home of the landlord we met Devi, the landlord's little son, who clapped his hands with joy and shouted to announce the coming of Chandu, the barber, in a beautiful heroic dress like that of the Padre Sahib of the Mission School.

"Ram! Ram! Ram!" said Bijay Chand, the burly landlord, touching the sacred thread which hung over his ear since he had just been to the lavatory. "The son of a pig! He is bringing a leather bag of cow-hide into our house and a coat of the marrow of, I don't know, some other animal, and those evil black Angrezi shoes. Get out! Get out! You son of a devil! You will defile my religion. I suppose you have no fear of anyone now that your father is dead!"

"But I am wearing the clothes of a Doctor, Jagirdar Sahib," said Chandu.

"Go away you, swine, go away and wear clothes befitting your low status as a barber, and don't let me see you practising any of your new-fangled notions, or else I will have you flogged!"

"But Rai Bijay Chand Sahib!" Chandu appealed.

"Get away! Get away! You useless one!" the landlord shouted. "Don't come any nearer, or we will have to treat the whole house with the sacred cow-dung to purify it."

Chandu returned. His face was flushed. He was completely

taken aback. He did not look at me because of the shame he
felt at being insulted before me whose hero he knew he was.
And he rushed towards the shop of Thanu Ram, the Sahukar
of the village, who kept a grocer's store at the corner of the
lane.

Devi, the landlord's son, had begun to cry at his father's
harsh words, and I stopped to quieten him. When I got to the
head of the lane I saw the Sahukar with one end of the scale
in which he had been weighing grain lifted in one hand,
abusing Chandu in the foulest way. "You little swine, you go
disguising yourself as a clown when you ought to be bearing
your responsibilities and looking after your old mother. You
go wearing the defiled clothes of the hospital folk! Go, and
come back in your own clothes! Then I shall let you cut my
hair!" And as he said so he felt for the ritual tuft knot on top
of his head.

Chandu looked very crestfallen, and ran in a wild rage past
me, as if I had been responsible for these mishaps. And I nearly
cried to think that he hated me now just because I belonged to
a superior caste.

"Go to Pandit Parmanand!" I shouted after him, "and tell
him that these garments you are wearing are not unclean."

"Ho, so you are in league with him," said Pandit Parmanand, emerging from the landlord's home, where he had
been apparently summoned to discuss this unholy emergency.
"You boys have been spoiled by the school education which
you have got. It may be all right for you to wear those things
because you are going to be a learned man, but what right has
that low-caste boy to such apparel? He has got to touch our
beards, our heads, and our hands. He is defiled enough by
God. Why does he want to become more defiled? You are a
high-caste boy. And he is a low-caste devil! He is a rogue!"

Chandu had heard this. He did not look back and ran in a
flurry, as if he were set on some purpose which occupied him
more than the abuse which had been the cause of his flight.

My mother called to me and said it was time for me to eat

32

and go to school, or I should be late. And she could not resist the temptation to lecture me again about my association with the barber boy.

But I was very disturbed about Chandu's fate all day, and, on my way back from school, I called in at the hovel where he lived with his mother.

His mother was well known for a cantankerous old woman, because she, a low-caste woman, dared to see the upper caste people as they never dared to see themselves. She was always very kind to me, though she spoke to me too in a bantering manner, which she had acquired through the suffering and humiliations of sixty-odd years. Turning to me she said, "Well, you have come, have you, to look for your friend. If your mother knew that you were here she would scratch my eyes out for casting my evil eye on your sweet face. And you, are you as innocent as you look or are you a sneaking little hypocrite like the rest of your lot?"

"Where is Chandu, then, mother?" I said.

"I don't know, son," she said, now in a sincere simple manner. "He went up town way and says he earned some money shaving people on the roadside. I don't know what he is up to. I don't think he ought to annoy the clients his father served. He is a child and gets funny notions into his head and they ought not to be angry with him. He is only a boy. You want to see him and go out playing, I suppose. Very well, I will tell him when he comes. He has just gone up the road, I think!"

"All right, mother," I said, and went home.

Chandu whistled for me that afternoon in the usual code whistle which we had arranged to evade the reproaches of interfering elders that our association often provoked.

"Come for a walk to the bazaar," he said. "I want to talk to you." And hardly had I joined him when he began: "Do you know. I earned a rupee shaving and hair-cutting near the court this morning. If I hadn't had to come back on the back bar of Hukam Chand's carriage early in the afternoon, I should have earned more. But I am going to teach these orthodox idiots a lesson. I am going on strike. I shall not go to their houses to attend to them. I am going to buy a Japanese bicycle from the gambling son of Lalla Hukam Chand for five rupees, and I shall learn to ride it and I will go to town on it every day. Won't I look grand, riding on a bicycle, with my overcoat, my black leather shoes, and a white turban on my head, specially as there is a peg in front of the two-wheeled carriage for hanging my tool-bag?"

"Yes," I agreed, greatly thrilled, not because I imagined the glory of Chandu seated on a bicycle, but because I felt myself nearer the goal of my ambition; since I felt that if Chandu acquired a bicycle he would at least let me ride to town on the elongated bolt at the back wheel or on the front bar, if he didn't let me learn to ride myself and lend me the machine every now and then.

Chandu negotiated the deal about the bicycle with an assurance that seemed to me a revelation of his capacity for business such as I had never suspected in him, from the reckless way he spent his money. And then he said to me in a confidential voice, "You wait for another day or two. I shall show you something which will make you laugh as you have never laughed before."

"Tell me now," I insisted, with an impatience sharpened by the rhythm of the excitement with which the spirit of his adventure filled my being.

"No, you wait," he said. "I can only give you a hint at the moment. It is a secret that only a barber can know. Now let me get on with job of learning to handle this machine. You hold it while I get on it, and I think it will be all right."

"But," I said, "this is not the way to learn to ride a bicycle. My father learned to ride from the peg at the back, and my brother learnt to ride by first trying to balance on the pedal."

"Your father is a top-heavy baboon!" said Chandu. "And your brother a long-legged spider."

"I," he continued, "was born, my mother tells me, upside down."

"All right," I said. And I held the bicycle for him. But while my gaze was concentrated with admiration on the brilliant sheen of the polished bars, I lost my grip and Chandu fell on the other side with a thud, along with the machine.

There were peals of laughter from the shop of the Sahukar, where several peasants congregated round the figure of the landlord. And then the Sahukar could be heard shouting, "Serve you right, you rascally son of the iron age! Break your bones and die, you upstart! You won't come to your senses otherwise!"

Chandu hung his head with shame, and muttered an oath at me, "You fool, you are no good!" though I had thought that he would grip me by the neck and give me a good thrashing for being the cause of his discomfiture. Then he looked at me, smiled embarrassedly, and said, "We will see who has the last laugh, I or they."

"I will hold the machine tightly this time," I said earnestly, and I picked it up from where it lay.

"Yes, break your bones, you swine," came the landlord's call.

"Don't you care!" Chandu said to me. "I will show them." And he mounted the bicycle as I exerted all my strength to hold it tight. Then he said, "Let go!"

I released my grip.

He had pressed the pedal with a downward pressure of his right foot, hard, and, as the wheels revolved, he swayed dangerously to one side. But he had pushed the other pedal now. The machine balanced, inclining to the right a little, so that I saw Chandu lift his rump from the saddle in the most frightening manner. He hung precariously for a moment. His handles wobbled dangerously. He was tottering. At this juncture a mixed noise of laughter and sarcasm arose from the congregation at the shop and I thought that Chandu would come to grief with this confusion, if not on account of

35

his utter incapacity. By a curious miracle, however, Chandu's feet had got into the right rhythm for pedalling and his handle had adjusted itself to his stiff hands, and he rode off with me running behind him, bursting myself with enthusiastic "Shabashes." A half mile run and he repeated the trick.

Though I was very eager to share the joy of his newly-acquired skill, I didn't see Chandu the next day, as I was being taken to see my aunts in Verka, straight from school.

But on the third day he called for me and said that he would show me the joke he had talked of the other day. I followed quickly, asking the while, "Tell me, what is it all about?"

"Look," he said, hiding behind the oven of the village potter. "Do you see the congregation of men in the Sahukar's shop? Try and see who's there."

I explored the various faces and, for a moment, I was quite baffled.

"Only the peasants sitting around waiting for the land-lord," I said.

"Look again, idiot," he said, "and see. The landlord is there, his long-jawed face dirtied by the white scum of his unshaved beard."

"Ha! Ha!" I shouted hilariously, struck by the contra-diction of the big thick moustache (which I knew the landlord dyed) with a prickly white bush on his jowls. "Ha! Ha!" I roared, "a sick lion! He looks seedy!"

"Sh!" warned Chandu. "Don't make a row! But look at the Sahukar. He looks like a leper with the brown tinge of tobacco on his walrus moustache which I once used to trim. Now you run past the shop and call 'Beavers, beavers!' They can't say anything to you!"

I was too impetuous a disciple of the impish Chandu to wait to deliberate.

"Beavers! Beavers! Beavers!" I shouted as I ran past the shop to the edge of the platform by the banyan tree.

The peasants who were gathered round the shop burst out

36

laughing, as they had apparently been itching to, for they had noticed the strong growths on the elders' faces, though they had not dared to say anything.

"Catch him, catch him, the little rogue!" shouted the Sahukar. "He is in league with that barber boy, Chandu!"

But, of course, I had climbed the banyan tree, from which I jumped on to the wall of the temple and shouted my slogan at the priest.

The rumour about the barber boy's strike spread, and jokes about the unkempt beards of the elders of the village became current in every home. Even those who were of high castes, even the members of the families of the elders, began to giggle with laughter at the shabby appearance of the great ones and made rude remarks about their persons. And it was said that at least the landlord's wife threatened to run away with some-body, because, being younger than her husband by twenty years, she had borne with him as long as he kept himself in trim, but was now disgusted with him beyond the limits of reconciliation.

Chandu did good business in town during these days and saved money, even though he bought new clothes and new tools for himself and gave me various presents.

The village elders threatened to have him sent to prison for his offences, and ordered his mother to force him to obey before they committed him to the police for a breach of the peace.

But Chandu's mother had for first time in her life touched the edge of prosperity, and she told them all what she thought of them in a language plainer than that in which she had always addressed them.

Then they thought of getting the barber of Verka to come and attend them, and offered him an anna instead of the two pice they usually paid to Chandu.

Chandu, however, had conceived a new notion this time, newer than those he had ever thought of before. Having seen the shop of Nringan Das, the barber of the town, he had

37

applied his brain to the scheme of opening a shop on the wayside at the head of the bazaar, in partnership with his cousin, the barber of Verka, and with Dhunoo and the other barbers within a range of seven miles from his village. He proposed his new idea to his cousin and Dhunoo and all the other barbers at a special meeting of his craft, and, by that gift of the gab which he had, besides his other qualities of Head and Heart, he convinced them all that it was time that the elders of the village came to them to be shaved rather than that they should dance attendance upon their lords and masters.

"Rajkot District Barber Brothers' Hairdressing and Shaving Saloon" has been followed by many other active trade unions of working men in our parts.

Sredni Vashtar

'SAKI'

CONRADIN was ten years old, and the doctor had pronounced his professional opinion that the boy would not live another five years. The doctor was silky and effete, and counted for little, but his opinion was endorsed by Mrs De Ropp, who counted for nearly everything. Mrs De Ropp was Conradin's cousin and guardian, and in his eyes she represented those three-fifths of the world that are necessary and disagreeable and real; the other two-fifths, in perpetual antagonism to the foregoing, were summed up in himself and his imagination. One of these days Conradin supposed he would succumb to the mastering pressure of wearisome necessary things—such as illnesses and coddling restrictions and drawn-out dullness. Without his imagination, which was rampant under the spur of loneliness, he would have succumbed long ago.

Mrs De Ropp would never, in her honestest moments, have confessed to herself that she disliked Conradin, though she might have been dimly aware that thwarting him "for his good" was a duty which she did not find particularly irksome. Conradin hated her with a desperate sincerity which he was perfectly able to mask. Such few pleasures as he could contrive for himself gained an added relish from the likelihood that they would be displeasing to his guardian, and from the realm of his imagination she was locked out—an unclean thing, which should find no entrance.

In the dull, cheerless garden, overlooked by so many windows that were ready to open with a message not to do this or that, or a reminder that medicines were due, he found little attraction. The few fruit-trees that it contained were set jealously apart from his plucking, as though they were rare specimens of their kind blooming in an arid waste; it would probably have been difficult to find a market-gardener who would have offered ten shillings for their entire yearly produce. In a forgotten corner, however, almost hidden behind a dismal shrubbery, was a disused tool-shed of respectable proportions, and within its walls Conradin found a haven, something that took on the varying aspects of a playroom and a cathedral. He had peopled it with a legion of familiar phantoms, evoked partly from fragments of history and partly from his own brain, but it also boasted two inmates of flesh and blood. In one corner lived a ragged-plumaged Houdan hen, on which the boy lavished an affection that had scarcely another outlet. Further back in the gloom stood a large hutch, divided into two compartments, one of which was fronted with close iron bars. This was the abode of a large polecat-ferret, which a friendly butcher-boy had once smuggled, cage and all, into its present quarters, in exchange for a long-secreted hoard of small silver. Conradin was dreadfully afraid of the lithe, sharp-fanged beast, but it was his most treasured possession. Its very presence in the tool-shed was a secret and fearful joy, to be kept scrupulously from the knowledge of the Woman, as he privately dubbed his cousin. And one day, out of Heaven knows what material, he spun the beast a wonderful name, and from that moment it grew into a god and a religion. The Woman indulged in religion once a week at a church near by, and took Conradin with her, but to him the church service was an alien rite in the House of Rimmon. Every Thursday, in the dim and musty silence of the tool-shed, he worshipped with mystic and elaborate ceremonial before the wooden hutch where dwelt Sredni Vashtar, the great ferret. Red flowers in their season and scarlet berries in the winter-time were offered at his shrine, for he was a god who laid some special stress on the fierce impatient side of things, as opposed to the Woman's religion, which, as far as Conradin could observe, went to great lengths in the contrary direction. And on great festivals powdered nutmeg was strewn in front of his hutch, an important feature of the offering being that the nutmeg had to be stolen. These festivals were of irregular occurrence, and were chiefly appointed to celebrate some passing event. On one occasion, when Mrs De Ropp suffered from acute toothache for three days, Conradin kept up the festival during the entire three days, and almost succeeded in persuading himself that Sredni Vashtar was personally responsible for the toothache. If the malady had lasted for another day the supply of nutmeg would have given out.

The Houdan hen was never drawn into the cult of Sredni Vashtar. Conradin had long ago settled that she was an Anabaptist. He did not pretend to have the remotest knowledge as to what an Anabaptist was, but he privately hoped that it was dashing and not very respectable. Mrs De Ropp was the ground plan on which he based and detested all respectability.

After a while Conradin's absorption in the tool-shed began to attract the notice of his guardian. "It is not good for him to be pottering down there in all weathers," she promptly decided, and at breakfast one morning she announced that the Houdan hen had been sold and taken away overnight. With her short-sighted eyes she peered at Conradin, waiting for an outbreak of rage and sorrow, which she was ready to rebuke with a flow of excellent precepts and reasoning. But Conradin said nothing: there was nothing to be said. Something perhaps in his white set face gave her a momentary qualm, for at tea that afternoon there was toast on the table, a delicacy which she usually banned on the ground that it was bad for him; also because the making of it "gave trouble", a deadly offence in the middle-class feminine eye.

"I thought you liked toast," she exclaimed, with an injured air, observing that he did not touch it.

"Sometimes," said Conradin.

In the shed that evening there was an innovation in the worship of the hutch-god. Conradin had been wont to chant his praises, tonight he asked a boon.

"Do one thing for me, Sredni Vashtar."

The thing was not specified. As Sredni Vashtar was a god he must be supposed to know. And choking back a sob as he looked at that other empty corner, Conradin went back to the world he so hated.

And every night, in the welcome darkness of his bedroom, and every evening in the dusk of the tool-shed, Conradin's bitter litany went up, "Do one thing for me, Sredni Vashtar."

Mrs De Ropp noticed that the visits to the shed did not cease, and one day she made a further journey of inspection.

"What are you keeping in that locked hutch?" she asked. "I believe it's guinea-pigs. I'll have them all cleared away."

Conradin shut his lips tight, but the Woman ransacked his bedroom till she found the carefully hidden key, and forthwith marched down to the shed to complete her discovery. It was a cold afternoon, and Conradin had been bidden to keep to the house. From the furthest window of the dining-room the door of the shed could just be seen beyond the corner of the shrubbery, and there Conradin stationed himself. He saw the Woman enter, and then he imagined her opening the door of the sacred hutch and peering down with her short-sighted eyes into the thick straw bed where his god lay hidden. Perhaps she would prod at the straw in her clumsy impatience. And Conradin fervently breathed his prayer for the last time. But he knew as he prayed that he did not believe. He knew that the Woman would come out presently with that pursed smile he loathed so well on her face, and that in an hour or two the gardener would carry away his wonderful god, a god no longer, but a simple brown ferret in a hutch. And he knew that the Woman would triumph always as she triumphed now, and that he would grow ever more sickly under her pestering and domineering and superior wisdom, till one day nothing would matter much more with him, and the doctor would be proved right. And in the sting and misery of his defeat, he began to chant loudly and defiantly the hymn of his threatened idol:

Sredni Vashtar went forth,
His thoughts were red thoughts and his teeth were white.
His enemies called for peace, but he brought them death.
Sredni Vashtar the Beautiful.

And then of a sudden he stopped his chanting and drew closer to the window-pane. The door of the shed still stood ajar as it had been left, and the minutes were slipping by. They were long minutes, but they slipped by nevertheless. He watched the starlings running and flying in little parties across the lawn; he counted them over and over again, with one eye always on that swinging door. A sour-faced maid came in to lay the table for tea, and still Conradin stood and waited and watched. Hope had crept by inches into his heart, and now a look of triumph began to blaze in his eyes that had only known the wistful patience of defeat. Under his breath, with a furtive exultation, he began once again the pæan of victory and devastation. And presently his eyes were rewarded: out through that doorway came a long, low, yellow-and-brown beast, with eyes a-blink at the waning daylight, and dark wet stains around the fur of jaws and throat. Conradin dropped on his knees. The great polecat-ferret made its way down to a small brook at the foot of the garden, drank for a moment, then crossed a little plank bridge and was lost to sight in the bushes. Such was the passing of Sredni Vashtar.

"Tea is ready," said the sour-faced maid; "where is the mistress?"

"She went down to the shed some time ago," said Conradin.

And while the maid went to summon her mistress to tea, Conradin fished a toasting-fork out of the sideboard drawer and proceeded to toast himself a piece of bread. And during the toasting of it and the buttering of it with much butter and the slow enjoyment of eating it, Conradin listened to the noises and silences which fell in quick spasms beyond the dining-room door. The loud foolish screaming of the maid, the answering chorus of wondering ejaculations from the kitchen region, the scuttering footsteps and hurried embassies for outside help, and then, after a lull, the scared sobbings and the shuffling tread of those who bore a heavy burden into the house.

"Whoever will break it to the poor child? I couldn't for the life of me!" exclaimed a shrill voice. And while they debated the matter among themselves, Conradin made himself another piece of toast.

A Story

DYLAN THOMAS

IF you can call it a story. There's no real beginning or end and there's very little in the middle. It is all about a day's outing, by charabanc, to Porthcawl, which, of course, the charabanc never reached, and it happened when I was so high and much nicer.

I was staying at the time with my uncle and his wife. Although she was my aunt, I never thought of her as anything but the wife of my uncle, partly because he was so big and trumpeting and red-hairy and used to fill every inch of the hot little house like an old buffalo squeezed into an airing cupboard, and partly because she was so small and silk and quick and made no noise at all as she whisked about on padded paws, dusting the china dogs, feeding the buffalo, setting the mousetraps that never caught her; and once she sleaked out of the room, to squeak in a nook or nibble in the hayloft, you forgot she had ever been there.

But there he was, always, a streaming hulk of an uncle, his braces straining like hawsers, crammed behind the counter of the tiny shop at the front of the house, and breathing like a brass band; or guzzling and blustery in the kitchen over his gutsy supper, too big for everything except the great black boats of his boots. As he ate, the house grew smaller; he billowed out over the furniture, the loud check meadow of his waistcoat littered, as though after a picnic, with cigarette ends, peelings, cabbage stalks, birds' bones, gravy; and the forest fire of his hair crackled among the hooked hams from the ceiling. She was so small she could hit him only if she stood on a chair, and every Saturday night at half-past ten he would lift her up, under his arm, on to a chair in the kitchen so that she could hit him on the head with whatever was handy, which was always a china dog. On Sundays, and when pickled, he sang high tenor, and had won many cups.

The first I heard of the annual outing was when I was sitting one evening on a bag of rice behind the counter, under one of my uncle's stomachs, reading an advertisement for sheep-dip, which was all there was to read. The shop was full of my uncle, and when Mr Benjamin Franklyn, Mr Weazley, Noah Bowen, and Will Sentry came in, I thought it would burst. It was like all being together in a drawer that smelt of cheese and turps, and twist tobacco and sweet biscuits and snuff and waistcoat. Mr Benjamin Franklyn said that he had collected enough money for the charabanc and twenty cases of pale ale and a pound apiece over that he would distribute among the members of the outing when they first stopped for refreshment, and he was about sick and tired, he said, of being followed by Will Sentry.

"All day long, wherever I go," he said, "he's after me like a collie with one eye. I got a shadow of my own *and* a dog. I don't need no Tom, Dick, or Harry pursuing me with his dirty muffler on."

Will Sentry blushed, and said, "It's only oily. I got a bicycle."

"A man has no privacy at all," Mr Franklyn went on. "I tell you he sticks so close I'm afraid to go out the back in case I sit in his lap. It's a wonder to me," he said, "he don't follow me into bed at night."

"Wife won't let," Will Sentry said.

And that started Mr Franklyn off again, and they tried to soothe him down by saying, "Don't you mind Will Sentry" ... "No harm in old Will" ... "He's only keeping an eye on the money, Benjie."

"Aren't I honest?" asked Mr Franklyn in surprise. There was no answer for some time, then Noah Bowen said, "You

46

know what the committee is. Ever since Bob the Fiddle they don't feel safe with a new treasurer."

"Do you think I'm going to drink the outing funds, like Bob the Fiddle did?" said Mr Franklyn.

"You *might*," said my uncle slowly.

"I resign," said Mr Franklyn.

"Not with our money you won't," Will Sentry said.

"Who put dynamite in the salmon pool?" said Mr Weazley, but nobody took any notice of him. And, after a time, they all began to play cards in the thickening dusk of the hot, cheesy shop, and my uncle blew and bugled whenever he won, and Mr Weazley grumbled like a dredger, and I fell to sleep on the gravy-scented mountain meadow of uncle's waistcoat.

On Sunday evening, after Bethesda, Mr Franklyn walked into the kitchen where my uncle and I were eating sardines with spoons from the tin because it was Sunday and his wife would not let us play draughts. She was somewhere in the kitchen, too. Perhaps she was inside the grandmother clock, hanging from the weights and breathing. Then, a second later, the door opened again and Will Sentry edged into the room, twiddling his hard, round hat. He and Mr Franklyn sat down on the settee, stiff and moth-balled and black in their chapel and funeral suits.

"I brought the list," said Mr Franklyn. "Every member fully paid. You ask Will Sentry."

My uncle put on his spectacles, wiped his whiskery mouth with a handkerchief big as a Union Jack, laid down his spoon of sardines, took Mr Franklyn's list of names, removed the spectacles so that he could read, and then ticked the names off one by one.

"Enoch Davies. Aye. He's good with his fists. You never know. Little Gerwain. Very melodious bass. Mr Cadwalladwr. That's right. He can tell opening time better than my watch. Mr Weazley. Of course. He's been to Paris. Pity he suffers so much in the charabanc. Stopped us nine times last year between the Beehive and the Red Dragon. Noah Bowen, ah,

47

very peaceable. He's got a tongue like a turtle-dove. Never a argument with Noah Bowen. Jenkins Loughor. Keep him off economics. It cost us a plate-glass window. And ten pints for the Sergeant. Mr Jervis. Very tidy."

"He tried to put a pig in the charra," Will Sentry said.

"Live and let live," said my uncle.

Will Sentry blushed.

"Sinbad the Sailor's Arms. Got to keep in with him. Old O. Jones."

"Why old O. Jones?" said Will Sentry.

"Old O. Jones always goes," said my uncle.

I looked down at the kitchen table. The tin of sardines was gone. By Gee, I said to myself, Uncle's wife is quick as a flash.

"Cuthbert Johnny Fortnight. Now there's a card," said my uncle.

"He whistles after women," Will Sentry said.

"So do you," said Mr Benjamin Franklyn, "in your mind."

My uncle at last approved the whole list, pausing only to say, when he came across one name, "If we weren't a Christian community, we'd chuck that Bob the Fiddle in the sea."

"We can do that in Porthcawl," said Mr Franklyn, and soon after that he went, Will Sentry no more than an inch behind him, their Sunday-bright boots squeaking on the kitchen cobbles.

And then, suddenly, there was my uncle's wife standing in front of the dresser, with a china dog in one hand. By Gee, I said to myself again, did you ever see such a woman, if that's what she is. The lamps were not lit yet in the kitchen and she stood in a wood of shadows, with the plates on the dresser behind her shining—like pink-and-white eyes.

"If you go on that outing on Saturday, Mr Thomas," she said to my uncle in her small, silk voice, "I'm going home to my mother's."

Holy Mo, I thought, she's got a mother. Now that's one old

48

bald mouse of a hundred and five I won't be wanting to meet in a dark lane.

"It's me or the outing, Mr Thomas."

I would have made my choice at once, but it was almost half a minute before my uncle said, "Well, then, Sarah, it's the outing, my love." He lifted her up, under his arm, on to a chair in the kitchen, and she hit him on the head with the china dog. Then he lifted her down again, and then I said good night.

For the rest of the week my uncle's wife whisked quiet and quick round the house with her darting duster, my uncle blew and bugled and swole, and I kept myself busy all the time being up to no good. And then at breakfast time on Saturday morning, the morning of the outing, I found a note on the kitchen table. It said, "There's some eggs in the pantry. Take your boots off before you go to bed." My uncle's wife had gone, as quick as a flash.

When my uncle saw the note, he tugged out the flag of his handkerchief and blew such a hubbub of trumpets that the plates on the dresser shook. "It's the same every year," he said. And then he looked at me. "But this year it's different. You'll have to come on the outing, too, and what the members will say I dare not think."

The charabanc drew up outside, and when the members of the outing saw my uncle and me squeeze out of the shop together, both of us cat-licked and brushed in our Sunday best, they snarled like a zoo.

"Are you bringing a *boy*?" asked Mr Benjamin Franklyn as we climbed into the charabanc. He looked at me with horror.

"Boys is nasty," said Mr Weazley.

"He hasn't paid his contributions," Will Sentry said.

"No room for boys. Boys get sick in charabancs."

"So do you, Enoch Davies," said my uncle.

"Might as well bring *women*."

The way they said it, women were worse than boys.

"Better than bringing grandfathers."

"Grandfathers is nasty too," said Mr Weazley.

"What can we do with him when we stop for refreshments?"

"I'm a grandfather," said Mr Weazley.

"Twenty-six minutes to opening time," shouted an old man in a panama hat, not looking at a watch. They forgot me at once.

"Good old Mr Cadwalladwr," they cried, and the charabanc started off down the village street.

A few cold women stood at their doorways, grimly watching us go. A very small boy waved goodbye, and his mother boxed his ears. It was a beautiful August morning.

We were out of the village, and over the bridge, and up the hill towards Steeplehat Wood when Mr Franklyn, with his list of names in his hand, called out loud, "Where's old O. Jones?"

"Where's old O?"

"We've left old O. behind."

"Can't go without old O."

And though Mr Weazley hissed all the way, we turned and drove back to the village, where, outside the Prince of Wales, old O. Jones was waiting patiently and alone with a canvas bag.

"I didn't want.to come at all," old O. Jones said as they hoisted him into the charabanc and clapped him on the back and pushed him on a seat and stuck a bottle in his hand, "but I always go." And over the bridge and up the hill and under the deep green wood and along the dusty road we wove, slow cows and ducks flying by, until "Stop the bus!" Mr Weazley cried. "I left my teeth on the mantelpiece."

"Never you mind," they said, "you're not going to bite nobody," and they gave him a bottle with a straw.

"I might want to smile," he said.

"Not you," they said.

"What's the time, Mr Cadwalladwr?"

"Twelve minutes to go," shouted back the old man in the panama, and they all began to curse him.

The charabanc pulled up outside the Mountain Sheep, a small, unhappy public-house with a thatched roof like a wig with ringworm. From a flagpole by the Gents fluttered the flag of Siam. I knew it was the flag of Siam because of cigarette cards. The landlord stood at the door to welcome us, simpering like a wolf. He was a long, lean, black-fanged man with a greased love-curl and pouncing eyes. "What a beautiful August day!" he said, and touched his love-curl with a claw. That was the way he must have welcomed the Mountain Sheep before he ate it, I said to myself. The members rushed out, bleating, and into the bar.

"You keep an eye on the charra," my uncle said; "see nobody steals it now."

"There's nobody to steal it," I said, "except some cows," but my uncle was gustily blowing his bugle in the bar. I looked at the cows opposite, and they looked at me. There was nothing else for us to do. Forty-five minutes passed, like a very slow cloud. The sun shone down on the lonely road, the lost, unwanted boy, and the lake-eyed cows. In the dark bar they were so happy they were breaking glasses. A Shoni-Onion Breton man, with a beret and a necklace of onions, bicycled down the road and stopped at the door.

"Quelle un grand matin, monsieur," I said.

"There's French, boy bach!" he said.

I followed him down the passage, and peered into the bar. I could hardly recognize the members of the outing. They had all changed colour. Beetroot, rhubarb, and puce, they hollered and rollicked in that dark, damp hole like enormous ancient bad boys, and my uncle surged in the middle, all red whiskers and bellies. On the floor was broken glass and Mr Weazley.

"Drinks all round," cried Bob the Fiddle, a small, absconding man with bright blue eyes and a plump smile.

"Who's been robbing the orphans?"

"Who sold his little babby to the gyppoes?"

"Trust old Bob, he'll let you down."

"You will have your little joke," said Bob the Fiddle, smiling like a razor, "but I forgive you, boys."

Out of the fug and babel I heard, "Come out and fight."

"No, not now, later."

"No, now when I'm in a temper."

"Look at Will Sentry, he's proper snobbled."

"Look at his wilful feet."

"Look at Mr Weazley lording it on the floor."

Mr Weazley got up, hissing like a gander. "That boy pushed me down deliberate," he said, pointing to me at the door, and I slunk away down the passage and out to the mild, good cows. Time clouded over, the cows wondered, I threw a stone at them and they wandered, wondering, away. Then out blew my uncle, ballooning, and one by one the members lumbered after him in a grizzle. They had drunk the Mountain Sheep dry. Mr Weazley had won a string of onions that the Shoni-Onion man raffled in the bar. "What's the good of onions if you left your teeth on the mantelpiece?" he said. And when I looked through the back window of the thundering charabanc, I saw the pub grow smaller in the distance. And the flag of Siam, from the flagpole by the Gents, fluttered now at half mast.

The Blue Bull, the Dragon, the Star of Wales, the Twll in the Wall, the Sour Grapes, the Shepherd's Arms, the Bells of Aberdovey: I had nothing to do in the whole, wild August world but remember the names where the outing stopped and keep an eye on the charabanc. And whenever it passed a public-house, Mr Weazley would cough like a billygoat and cry, "Stop the bus, I'm dying of breath!" And back we would all have to go.

Closing time meant nothing to the members of that outing. Behind locked doors, they hymned and rumpused all the beautiful afternoon. And, when a policeman entered the Druid's Tap by the back door, and found them all choral with beer, "Sssh!" said Noah Bowen, "the pub is shut."

"Where do you come from?" he said in his buttoned, blue voice.

They told him.

"I got a auntie there," the policeman said. And very soon he was singing "Asleep in the Deep."

Off we drove again at last, the charabanc bouncing with tenors and flagons, and came to a river that rushed along among willows.

"Water!" they shouted.

"Porthcawl!" sang my uncle.

"Where's the donkeys?" said Mr Weazley.

And out they lurched, to paddle and whoop in the cool, white, winding water. Mr Franklyn, trying to polka on the slippery stones, fell in twice. "Nothing is simple," he said with dignity as he oozed up the bank.

"It's cold!" they cried.

"It's lovely!"

"It's smooth as a moth's nose!"

"It's *better* than Porthcawl!"

And dusk came down warm and gentle on thirty wild, wet, pickled, splashing men without a care in the world at the end of the world in the west of Wales. And, "Who goes there?" called Will Sentry to a wild duck flying.

They stopped at the Hermit's Nest for a rum to keep out the cold. "I played for Aberavon in 1898," said a stranger to Enoch Davies.

"Liar," said Enoch Davies.

"I can show you photos," said the stranger.

"Forged," said Enoch Davies.

"And I'll show you my cap at home."

"Stolen."

"I got friends to prove it," the stranger said in a fury.

"Bribed," said Enoch Davies.

On the way home, through the simmering moon-splashed dark, old O. Jones began to cook his supper on a primus stove in the middle of the charabanc. Mr Weazley coughed himself blue in the smoke. "Stop the bus," he cried, "I'm dying of breath!" We all climbed down into the moonlight. There was not a public-house in sight. So they carried out the remaining cases, and the primus stove, and old O. Jones himself, and took them into a field, and sat down in a circle in the field and drank and sang while old O. Jones cooked sausage and mash and the moon flew above us. And there I drifted to sleep against my uncle's mountainous waistcoat, and, as I slept, "Who goes there?" called out Will Sentry to the flying moon.

Thithyphuth, or my
Uncle's Waiter

WOLFGANG BORCHERT

NOT, of course, that my uncle managed a pub. But he did know a waiter. This waiter dogged my uncle with such devotion and respect that we always said, "That's his waiter," or, "Ah, *his* waiter".

I was present when my uncle and the waiter became acquainted. I was then just big enough to rest my nose on the table. This I was only allowed to do if it—my nose—was clean. And of course it was not always clean. My mother too was not much older. She was necessarily somewhat older, but we were both so young that we were quite horrified when my uncle and the waiter met. Yes, my mother and I were there.

And my uncle of course, likewise the waiter, for the pair were destined to meet, and so it came to pass. My mother and I were only there as extras and we afterwards bitterly rued our presence, for really we could only be very ashamed when the pair's acquaintance began. In point of fact it led to all sorts of frightful scenes, with insults, complaints, laughter, and shouting. And there was almost a free fight. That my uncle had a speech defect was very nearly the occasion of this brawl. That he had only one leg finally prevented it.

So we three, my uncle, my mother, and myself, sat one sunny summer afternoon in a large, resplendent, gay beer-garden. Around us sat about two or three hundred other people, all perspiring. Dogs lay in the shade of the tables and wasps settled on the plates of cakes. Or circled round the children's lemonade glasses. It was so hot and full that the waiters all wore injured looks, as though it were all a conspiracy. One of them at last came over to our table.

Now, as I was saying, my uncle had a speech defect. Not considerable, but nevertheless distinct enough. He couldn't pronounce an "s". Nor a "z" or "tz". He simply couldn't do it. When a hard "s" sound came up in a word, he came out with a weak, damp, watery 'th'. And in so doing he pursed his lips out so that his mouth bore a faint resemblance to a hen's backside.

Well, the waiter stood at our table, and flicked the cake-crumbs of our predecessors from the cloth with his handkerchief. (It was many years later that I learned that this must have been not his handkerchief but a kind of napkin.) So he flicked about with it and asked, short-breathed and nervous,

"Yeth pleath? Would you like thomething?"

My uncle, who had no love for non-alcoholic drinks, replied in his habitual way,

"Let'th thee. Two brandieth. And for the child a fithy drink or lemonade-thoda. Or what elthe have you?"

The waiter was very pale. And yet it was midsummer, and he was a waiter in a beer-garden. But perhaps he was overworked. And I suddenly noticed that under his clear brown skin my uncle had also turned pale. Actually, this was when the waiter repeated the order to confirm it,

"Very good. Two brandieth. A thoda. Thank you."

My uncle looked at my mother with raised eyebrows, as if he expected something cogent from her. But he only wanted to reassure himself that he was still in this world. Then, in a voice reminiscent of the distant thunder of guns, he said,

"Jutht tell me, are you crathy? You? You're making fun of my lithp, eh?"

The waiter stood there, and then he began to tremble. His hands trembled. His eyelids. His knees. But above all his voice trembled. It trembled in pain and anger and incomprehension as he endeavoured to reply somewhat in the thunder-of-guns manner,

"It'th thcandalouth of you to amuthe yourthelf at my expenthe, it'th dithrethpectful, if you pleath."

Now he trembled all over. The tails of his jacket. His smarmed-down strands of hair. His nostrils and his scant lower lip.

No part of my uncle shook. I looked at him scrupulously; absolutely no part. I admired my uncle. But when the waiter called him scandalous, then at last my uncle stood up. That is to say, he by no means stood up properly speaking. With his one leg, that would have been much too formal and difficult. He remained seated and nevertheless stood up. He stood up within himself. Which, too, was perfectly adequate. The waiter felt this inner rising of my uncle's like an offensive, and he fell back a couple of short, shaky, uncertain steps. Hostile, they stood facing one another. Although my uncle sat. If he really had stood up, the waiter would probably have sat down. And my uncle could afford to remain seated, for seated he was as large as the waiter, and their heads were on the same level.

So now they stood and looked at each other. Both with a too-short tongue, both with the same deficiency. But each with a completely different destiny.

Little, embittered, toil-worn, preoccupied, fidgety, pale, cowed, crushed: the waiter. The little waiter. A genuine waiter: sullen, conventionally polite, odourless, faceless, numbered, scrubbed yet ever so slightly scruffy. A little waiter. Nicotine-fingered, servile, sterile, bland, well-combed, blue-shaven, fed up to the teeth, nothing to fill his trousers with

57

behind and bulging pockets either side, down-at-heel and with a perpetually sweat-stained collar—the little waiter.

And my uncle? Oh, my uncle! Broad, brown, bumbling, bass-voiced, loud, laughing, living, copious, colossal, calm, secure, satisfied, salacious—my uncle!

The little waiter and my large uncle. Different as a dray-horse and a dirigible. But both short-tongued. Both with the same defect. Both with a damp, watery, weak 'th'. But the waiter a pariah, down-trodden by his fatal tongue, mutinous, intimidated, disappointed, lonely, testy.

And become quite, quite small. Ridiculed a thousand times a day, smiled at, laughed at, pitied, smirked at, and bawled at from every table. A thousand times every day at every table in the beer-garden retracting a centimetre within himself, humbled and crumpled. A thousand times every day at every order at every table, at every 'pleath', becoming ever smaller and smaller. The tongue, that giant, amorphous lobe of flesh, the much-too-short tongue, that shapeless cyclopean lump of flesh, that unwieldy, incompetent, red conglomeration of muscle, that tongue had reduced him to a pygmy: little, little waiter!

And my uncle! But with a too-short tongue; as if he had none. My uncle, laughing loudest himself when he was laughed at. My uncle, one-legged, gigantic, lisp-tongued. But an Apollo in every inch of his body and every atom of his soul. Car driver, woman driver, man driver, racing driver. My uncle, boozer, singer, strong-arm man, joke merchant, smut-mutterer, seducer, short-tongued spraying sputtering spitting devotee of women and brandy. My uncle, carousing conqueror, artificial limb creaking, broad-grinning, with his much-too-short tongue, though; as if he had none.

So they stood facing one another. Murderous and mortally wounded the one, jovial and brimming with explosive laughter the other. All around, six to seven hundred eyes and ears, saunterers, coffee-drinkers, cake-guzzlers, who enjoyed the scene more than beer, fizz, and honey-cakes. Oh, and my mother and I in the middle of it all. Red to the roots, ashamed, cringing into our clothes. And this was only the beginning of our sorrows.

"Pleath find the landlord at onthe, you aggrethive thparrow, you. I'll teatth you to inthult cuthtomerth."

My uncle now spoke so purposefully loud that the six to seven hundred ears missed not a word. The brandy pleasantly stimulated him. He grinned with delight all over his great, genial, broad, brown face. Shining salty pearls broke out on his brow and rolled down over the massive cheekbones. But the waiter took this in him for malevolence, mean trickery, insult, and provocation. He stood there with puckered, hollow, slightly quivering cheeks and did not move from the spot.

"Have you got thand in your ear-holth? Call the owner, you thothled thimpleton. Off with you, or have you thit your-thelf, you miththapen thprite?"

Then the little pygmy, the little lisp-tongued waiter, took courage—a magnanimous, huge courage, surprising for us all and for himself. He stepped up quite close to our table, flicked over our plates with his handkerchief and bowed a correct waiter's bow. With a tiny, masculine, decisive, and low voice, with an overwhelming, trembling politeness, he said, "If you pleath!" and sat, brief, bold, nonchalant, on the free, fourth chair at our table. Of course only simulated nonchalance. For in his brave little waiter's heart there flared the rebellious flame of a creature despised, frightened, misshapen. And yet he had not the courage to look at my uncle. He merely sat down, so small and pertinent, and I think that at the most an eighth of his bottom was in contact with the chair. (If he had more than an eighth at all—out of sheer modesty.) He sat, looked in front of him at the grey-white coffee-spotted table-cloth, drew out his bulky wallet and laid it on the table, still something of a man. He risked a brief look up for half a second, although he had already gone too far by plumping down his wallet, then, when he saw that the mountain, i.e. my uncle, persisted in its immovableness, he opened the wallet and drew out a piece of clipped-up cardboard-like paper, whose folds showed the characteristic yellow of a well-worn piece of paper. He snapped it open with much ado, dispensed with any expression of being the injured party or of seeking redress, and pointedly laid his stubby, worn finger on a particular place of the piece of paper. He added softly, a mite more hoarse and with long pauses for breath,

"Pleath. If you would pleath look. Motht courteouth if you would make thertain for yourthelf. My pathport. Been in Parith. Barthelona. Othnabrück, pleath. Thee it all in my pathport. And here—Thpethial Peculiaritieth—thcar on left knee (from playing thoccer). And here, here? What'th thith here? Here, pleath: Thpeech defect thinth birth. If you pleath. Ath you can thee for yourthelf!"

Life had treated him too uncharitably for him now to have the courage to enjoy his triumph to the full and challenge my uncle with a look. No, still and small, he looked at his outstretched finger and the demonstrable born defect and waited patiently for my uncle's bass.

It was not long in coming. And when it came, what he said was so unexpected that I hiccupped with fright. My uncle, with his clumsy, four-square, man-of-action hands, suddenly seized the tiny fluttering paws of the waiter and said, with the vital, power-and-fury bonhomie and warm animal tenderness which is the primary characteristic of all giants, "Poor little beatht! Have they been baiting you ever thinth birth?"

The waiter gulped. Then he nodded. Nodded six, seven times. Saved. Satisfied. Proud. Out of danger. He could not speak. He comprehended nothing. Understanding and speech were choked by two ample tears. Nor could he see, for the two fat tears rose before his pupils like two opaque, all-appeasing curtains. He comprehended nothing. But his heart received this wave of sympathy like a desert that had waited a thousand

60

years for an ocean. He could have let himself be flooded over like this to the end of his life; until death he could have hidden his tiny hands in my uncle's clutches. Unto eternity he could have listened to this, "Poor little beatht!"

But all this was going on too long for my uncle. He drove a car. Even when sitting in a pub. He let his voice boom out like a salvo of artillery over the beer-garden and thundered at some terrified waiter,

"You there, waiter! Eight brandieth! And tharp about it, I thay. What? Not your table? Eight brandieth at onthe, or do you refuthe, eh?"

The unknown waiter looked at my uncle, browbeaten and flabbergasted. Then at his colleague, who could readily have indicated by eye (by a wink or the like) what it was all about. But the little waiter could scarcely recognize this colleague, so far was he from all that bore the name of waiter, cake-plate, coffee-cup, and colleague, far, far from it.

Next, the eight brandies stood on the table. Immediately the strange waiter had to gather four glasses from it, which were empty before he had time to draw one breath. "Fill 'em up onthe more!" ordered my uncle, and rummaged in the inside pocket of his jacket. Then he whistled a note that shot through the air and laid, for his part, his bulky wallet next to that of his new friend. He eventually fumbled out a dog-eared card and put his middle finger, which was as thick as a child's arm, on a specific part of it.

"You thee, you thtupid little donkey, here it ith: leg amputathion and lower maxillary wound. War wound." And as he spoke, he pointed out with his other hand a scar which lay concealed under his chin.

"The bathtardth thimply thot a pieth off the tip of my tongue. In Franthe, it wath."

The waiter nodded.

"Thtill upthet?" my uncle asked.

The waiter shook his head rapidly to and fro, as if he wanted to ward off something totally impossible.

"I only thought at firtht you wanted to teathe me."

Shattered by his mistake in understanding human nature, he continued to wag his head from left to right and back again.

And now it seemed as if at once he had shaken off all the tragedy of his fate. The two tears, which now coursed down the hollows of his face, took with them all the torment of his hitherto derided existence. The new era in his life, on which he entered in my uncle's giant paw, began with a tiny, erupting laugh, a titter, timid, bashful, but accompanied by an unmistakable stench of brandy.

And my uncle, that uncle who laughed his way through life with one leg, a shot-up tongue, and a bear-like bass-voiced sense of humour, that uncle of mine was now so unbelievably happy that he finally, finally was able to laugh. By now he had blushed so bronze that I feared he might burst at any moment. And his laughter laughed out, tremendously; exploded, rumbled, huzza'd, resounded, gurgled—laughed as if he were a giant saurian from whom these primeval noises belched forth. The first little tentative man's laugh of the waiter, of the new little waiter-man, was, by contrast, like the thin snuffling of a cold-nipped kid goat. Anxiously I groped for my mother's hand. Not that I was frightened of my uncle, but I had a deep animal apprehension of the eight brandies that fomented within him. My mother's hand was ice-cold. All the blood had drained up from her body to turn her head into a glaring advertising symbol of modesty and middle-class morality. No prize tomato could radiate a redder red. My mother shone. Poppies were pale beside her. I slid from my chair beneath the table. All around us, seven hundred pairs of eyes were round and huge. Oh, how ashamed we were, my mother and I!

Thithyphuth, or my Uncle's Waiter

The little waiter, who had become a new man under the hot alcoholic breath of my uncle, apparently wished to start the first part of his new life with a period of goatish bleating laughter. He baa'd and bleated, gaggled and guggled like a whole flock of lambs at once. And as the two men now knocked back four more additional brandies over their short tongues, out of the lambs, out of the pink thin-voiced soft shy little waiter-lambs there grew quite mighty rough-hewn bleating primordial white-bearded metal-clattering rubbish- blattering rams.

This metamorphosis from the tiny venomous numb pinched misery to the persistent, prolonged bleating thigh-slapping racketing raucous rattling he-goat was strange even to my uncle. His laughter gurgled away like a stanched waterfall. He wiped the tears from his brown broad face with his sleeve and goggled with brandy-bright staring astonished eyes at the white-jacketed dwarf waiter rocking with quakes of laughter. Seven hundred faces were grinning all round us. Seven hundred pairs of eyes could not believe what they saw. Seven hundred midriffs were in agony. Those who sat farthest away stood up excitedly so that nothing escaped them. It was as if the waiter had resolved to pursue his life henceforth as a gigantic wicked bleating ram. And just now, after being submerged in his own laughter for a few minutes as though pent up, just now, in between the salvoes of laughter that sparkled from his round mouth like metallic machine-gun fire, he succeeded in ejecting short shrill shrieks. He managed to retain so much breath between the laughs that he could now whinny these cries into the air.

"Thithyphuth!" he cried and slapped his damp brow. "Thithyphuth! Thiiithyyyphuuuth!" He took a firm hold of the table-top with both hands and neighed: "Thithyphuth!" After he had neighed about a couple of dozen times, had neighed this. "Thithyphuth" exultantly, the "thithyphuths" became too much for my uncle. He crumpled the starched

63

shirt of the ceaselessly neighing waiter in one single grip, hammered the other fist on the table so that twelve empty glasses began to dance, and thundered at him, "Thtop! Thtop it, I thay. What'th thith thilly thtupid Thithyphuth mean? Thtop it now, do you underthtand!"

The grip and my uncle's thundering bass turned the thithyphuth-crying he-goat into the tiny lisping wretched waiter again in one and the same moment.

He stood up. He stood up as if it had been the greatest mistake of his life to have sat down. He brushed his napkin over his face and cleared away tears of laughter, beads of perspiration, brandy, and hilarity like things of the past that were accursed and wanton. But he was so drunk that he took it all for a dream—the familiarity at the outset, the suffering, and the friendship of my uncle. He was in doubt: have I just cried "Thithyphuth"? Or not? Have I knocked back thix brandieth, I, the waiter of thith pub, in the middle of my cuthtomerth? Me? He was not sure. And in any case he made a little truncated bow and whispered "Thorry!" And then he bowed again, "Thorry. Yeth, pleath forgive the 'Thithyphuth' cry. If you pleath. Would the gentleman pleath forgive me if I wath too loud, but the brandieth, ath you mutht know yourthelf, if you haven't eaten anything, on an empty thtomach. Tho pleath. 'Thithyphuth' was actually my nickname. Yeth, at thcool. The whole clath called me that. You mutht know that Thithyphuth wath the man in hell, thith old myth, you know, of the man in Hadeth, the poor thinner, who was thuppothed to puth a great thtone up a huge mountain, ah, had to, yeth, that wath Thithyphuth, ath you know. I alwayth had to tell thith in thcool, alwayth thith Thithyphuth. And they all burtht with laughter then, ath you may well imagine, my good thir. They all laughed, you know, thinthe I had the tip of my tongue too thort. Tho it came about that later on I wath called Thithyphuth everywhere and wath teathed, you thee. And that, thorry, thprang tho much into my mind with the brandieth, when I thouted out tho, you underthtand. Forgive me, pleath, forgive me if I have bothered you, pleath."

He fell silent. His napkin in the meanwhile had passed from one hand to the other countless times. Then he looked at my uncle.

Now it was his turn to sit still at the table and look down at the table-cloth. He dare not look at the waiter. My uncle, my bearish, bullish giant uncle dare not raise his eyes and counter the look of this little self-conscious waiter. And the two full tears that now welled in his eyes. But no one except me saw that. And I only saw it because I was so small that I could look up into his face from below. He pushed an extravagant banknote over to the motionless, expectant waiter, impatiently waved him off when he wanted to give it back, and stood up without looking at anyone.

The waiter, timid still, produced another sentence: "The brandieth I would have liked to have paid for mythelf, if you pleath."

However, he had already put the note in his wallet, as though he expected no answer and no protest. Moreover, no one had heard the sentence and his generosity fell silently on the hard gravel of the beer-garden and was there later trampled indifferently underfoot. My uncle took his stick, we stood up, my mother supported my uncle and we went slowly out to the street. None of us three looked at the waiter. Not my mother and I, because we were ashamed. Not my uncle, for he had those two tears in his eyes. Perhaps he was ashamed too, this uncle. Slowly we approached the exit; my uncle's stick crunched nastily in the garden gravel, and this was the only sound for the moment, for the three to four hundred faces at the tables were concentrated, mute and goggle-eyed, on our departure.

And suddenly I felt sorry for the little waiter. As we were about to turn the corner at the beer-garden exit, I looked quickly round at him once again. He was still standing at our table. His white napkin hung down to the ground. He seemed to me to have become much, much smaller. He stood there so small, and I loved him suddenly when I saw him stare our way, so forsaken behind us, so small, so grey, so empty, so poor, so cold, and so immensely alone! Oh, how small! He gave me such infinite pain that I was moved to tap my uncle's hand, and I said quietly, "I think he is crying now."

My uncle stopped. He looked at me and I could make out the two full tears in his eyes quite clearly. I said yet again, without fully understanding why I really did it, "Oh, he's crying. Just look, he's crying."

Then my uncle let go of my mother's arm, hobbled a couple of swift, solid steps back, heaved his crutch high like a sword and stabbed into the sky with it and bellowed with the whole grand power of his mighty body and his lungs,

"Thithyphuth! Thithyphuth! Can you hear? *Au revoir*, old Thithyphuth! Till nextht Thunday, poor beatht! Wiederthehen!"

The two full tears were crushed to nothing by the wrinkles that now spread over his good brown features. They were creases of laughter and his whole face was full of them. Once again he swept the skies with his crutch, as if he wanted to rake down the sun, and again his giant laughter thundered away over the beer-garden tables, "Thithyphuth! Thithyphuth!"

And Thithyphuth, the poor little grey waiter, awoke from the dead, raised his napkin and worked it up and down like a window-cleaner gone beserk. He wiped away the whole grey world, all the beer-gardens of the world, all waiters, and all the speech-defects of the world with his waving, finally and for ever out of his life. And he shouted back, shrill and overjoyed, standing on tiptoe, without interrupting his window-cleaning,

"I underthtand! Yeth pleath! On Thunday! Yeth, *au revoir!* On Thunday, pleath!"

Then we turned the corner. My uncle caught hold of my mother's arm again and said softly, "I know it wath quite dreadful for you. But what elthe could I do, tell me that? Thuch a thilly donkey. Running around all hith life with a nathty thpeech impediment like that. Poor beatht!"

Casting the Runes

M. R. JAMES

April 15th.

Dear Sir,—I am requested by the Council of the —— Association to return to you the draft of a paper on *The Truth of Alchemy,* which you have been good enough to offer to read at our forthcoming meeting, and to inform you that the Council do not see their way to including it in the programme.

I am,
Yours faithfully,
—— *Secretary.*

April 18th.

Dear Sir,—I am sorry to say that my engagements do not permit of my affording you an interview on the subject of your proposed paper. Nor do our laws allow of your discussing the matter with a Committee of our Council, as you suggest. Please allow me to assure you that the fullest consideration was given to the draft which you submitted, and that it was not declined without having been referred to the judgment of a most competent authority. No personal question (it can hardly be necessary for me to add) can have had the slightest influence on the decision of the Council.

Believe me (*ut supra*).

April 20th.

The Secretary of the —— Association begs respectfully to inform Mr Karswell that it is impossible for him to communicate the name of any person or persons to whom the draft of Mr Karswell's paper may have been submitted; and further desires to intimate that he cannot undertake to reply to any further letters on this subject.

"And who is Mr Karswell?" inquired the Secretary's wife. She had called at his office, and (perhaps unwarrantably) had picked up the last of these three letters, which the typist had just brought in.

"Why, my dear, just at present Mr Karswell is a very angry man. But I don't know much about him otherwise, except that he is a person of wealth, his address is Lufford Abbey, Warwickshire, and he's an alchemist, apparently, and wants to tell us all about it; and that's about all—except that I don't want to meet him for the next week or two. Now, if you're ready to leave this place, I am."

"What have you been doing to make him angry?" asked Mrs Secretary.

"The usual thing, my dear, the usual thing: he sent in a draft of a paper he wanted to read at the next meeting, and we referred it to Edward Dunning—almost the only man in England who knows about these things—and he said it was perfectly hopeless so we declined it. So Karswell has been pelting me with letters ever since. The last thing he wanted was the name of the man we referred his nonsense to; you saw my answer to that. But don't you say anything about it, for goodness' sake."

"I should think not, indeed. Did I ever do such a thing? I do hope, though, he won't get to know that it was poor Mr Dunning."

"Poor Mr Dunning? I don't know why you call him that; he's a very happy man, is Dunning. Lots of hobbies and a comfortable home, and all his time to himself."

"I only meant I should be sorry for him if this man got hold of his name, and came and bothered him."

"Oh, ah! yes. I dare say he would be poor Mr Dunning then."

The Secretary and his wife were lunching out, and the friends to whose house they were bound were Warwickshire people. So Mrs Secretary had already settled it in her own mind that she would question them judiciously about Mr Karswell. But she was saved the trouble of leading up to the subject, for the hostess said to the host, before many minutes had passed, "I saw the Abbot of Lufford this morning." The host whistled. "*Did* you? What in the world brings him up to town?" "Goodness knows; he was coming out of the British Museum gate as I drove past." It was not unnatural that Mrs Secretary should inquire whether this was a real Abbot who was being spoken of. "Oh no, my dear: only a neighbour of ours in the country who bought Lufford Abbey a few years ago. His real name is Karswell." "Is he a friend of yours?" asked Mr Secretary, with a private wink to his wife. The question let loose a torrent of declamation. There was really nothing to be said for Mr Karswell. Nobody knew what he did with himself: his servants were a horrible set of people; he had invented a new religion for himself, and practised no one could tell what appalling rites; he was very easily offended, and never forgave anybody: he had a dreadful face (so the lady insisted, her husband somewhat demurring); he never did a kind action, and whatever influence he did exert was mischievous. "Do the poor man justice, dear," the husband interrupted. "You forget the treat he gave the school children." "Forget it, indeed! But I'm glad you mentioned it, because it gives an idea of the man. Now, Florence, listen to this. The first winter he was at Lufford this delightful neighbour of ours wrote to the clergyman of his parish (he's not ours, but we know him very well) and offered to show the school children some magic-lantern slides. He said he had some new kinds, which he thought would interest them. Well, the clergyman was rather surprised, because Mr Karswell had shown himself inclined to be unpleasant to the children—complaining of their trespassing, or something of the sort; but of course he accepted, and the evening was fixed, and our friend went himself to see that everything went right. He said he never had been so thankful for anything as that his own children were all prevented from being there: they were at a children's party at our house, as a matter of fact. Because this Mr Karswell had evidently set out with the intention of frightening these poor village children out of their wits, and I do believe, if he had been allowed to go on, he would actually have done so. He began with some comparatively mild things. Red Riding Hood was one, and even then, Mr Farrer said, the wolf was so dreadful that several of the smaller children had to be taken out: and he said Mr Karswell began the story by producing a noise like a wolf howling in the distance, which was the most gruesome thing he had ever heard. All the slides he showed, Mr Farrer said, were most clever; they were absolutely realistic, and where he had got them or how he worked them he could not imagine. Well, the show went on, and the stories kept on becoming a little more terrifying each time, and the children were mesmerized into complete silence. At last he produced a series which represented a little boy passing through his own park—Lufford, I mean—in the evening. Every child in the room could recognize the place from the pictures. And this poor boy was followed, and at last pursued and overtaken, and either torn in pieces or somehow made away with, by a horrible hopping creature in white, which you saw first dodging about among the trees, and gradually it appeared more and more plainly. Mr Farrer said it gave him one of the worst nightmares he ever remembered, and what it must have meant to the children doesn't bear thinking of. Of course this was too much, and he spoke very sharply indeed to Mr Karswell, and said it couldn't go on. All *he* said was, 'Oh, you think it's time to bring our little show to an end and

71

send them home to their beds? *Very* well!' And then, if you please, he switched on another slide, which showed a great mass of snakes, centipedes, and disgusting creatures with wings, and somehow or other he made it seem as if they were climbing out of the picture and getting in amongst the audience; and this was accompanied by a sort of dry rustling noise which sent the children nearly mad, and of course they stampeded. A good many of them were rather hurt in getting out of the room, and I don't suppose one of them closed an eye that night. There was the most dreadful trouble in the village afterwards. Of course the mothers threw a good part of the blame on poor Mr Farrer, and, if they could have got past the gates, I believe the fathers would have broken every window in the Abbey. Well, now, that's Mr Karswell: that's the Abbot of Lufford, my dear, and you can imagine how we covet *his* society."

"Yes, I think he has all the possibilities of a distinguished criminal, has Karswell," said the host. "I should be sorry for anyone who got into his bad books."

"Is he the man, or am I mixing him up with someone else?" asked the Secretary (who for some minutes had been wearing the frown of the man who is trying to recollect something). "Is he the man who brought out a *History of Witchcraft* some time back—ten years or more?"

"That's the man; do you remember the reviews of it?"

"Certainly I do; and what's equally to the point, I knew the author of the most incisive of the lot. So did you: you must remember John Harrington; he was at John's in our time."

"Oh, very well indeed, though I don't think I saw or heard anything of him between the time I went down and the day I read the account of the inquest on him."

"Inquest?" said one of the ladies. "What has happened to him?"

"Why, what happened was that he fell out of a tree and broke his neck. But the puzzle was, what could have induced

72

him to get up there. It was a mysterious business, I must say. Here was this man—not an athletic fellow, was he? and with no eccentric twist about him that was ever noticed—walking home along a country road late in the evening—no tramps about—well known and liked in the place—and he suddenly begins to run like mad, loses his hat and stick, and finally shins up a tree—quite a difficult tree—growing in the hedgerow: a dead branch gives way, and he comes down with it and breaks his neck, and there he's found next morning with the most dreadful face of fear on him that could be imagined. It was pretty evident, of course, that he had been chased by something, and people talked of savage dogs, and beasts escaped out of menageries; but there was nothing to be made of that. That was in '89, and I believe his brother Henry (whom I remember as well at Cambridge, but *you* probably don't) has been trying to get on the track of an explanation ever since. He, of course, insists there was malice in it, but I don't know. It's difficult to see how it could have come in."

After a time the talk reverted to the *History of Witchcraft.* "Did you ever look into it?" asked the host.

"Yes, I did," said the Secretary. "I went so far as to read it."

"Was it as bad as it was made out to be?"

"Oh, in point of style and form, quite hopeless. It deserved all the pulverizing it got. But, besides that, it was an evil book. The man believed every word of what he was saying, and I'm very much mistaken if he hadn't tried the greater part of his receipts."

"Well, I only remember Harrington's review of it, and I must say if I'd been the author it would have quenched my literary ambition for good. I should never have held up my head again."

"It hasn't had the effect in the present case. But come, it's half-past three; I must be off."

On the way home the Secretary's wife said, "I do hope that horrible man won't find out that Mr Dunning had anything to do with the rejection of his paper." "I don't think there's much chance of that," said the Secretary. "Dunning won't mention it himself, for these matters are confidential, and none of us will for the same reason. Karswell won't know his name, for Dunning hasn't published anything on the same subject yet. The only danger is that Karswell might find out, if he was to ask the British Museum people who was in the habit of consulting alchemical manuscripts: I can't very well tell them not to mention Dunning, can I? It would set them talking at once. Let's hope it won't occur to him."

However, Mr Karswell was an astute man.

This much is in the way of prologue. On an evening rather later in the same week, Mr Edward Dunning was returning from the British Museum, where he had been engaged in Research, to the comfortable house in a suburb where he lived alone, tended by two excellent women who had been long with him. There is nothing to be added by way of description of him to what we have heard already. Let us follow him as he takes his sober course homewards.

A train took him to within a mile or two of his house, and an electric tram a stage farther. The line ended at a point some three hundred yards from his front door. He had had enough of reading when he got into the car, and indeed the light was not such as to allow him to do more than study the advertisements on the panes of glass that faced him as he sat. As was not unnatural, the advertisements in this particular line of cars were objects of his frequent contemplation, and, with the possible exception of the brilliant and convincing dialogue between Mr Lamplough and an eminent K.C. on the subject of Pyretic Saline, none of them afforded much scope to his imagination. I am wrong: there was one at the corner of the car farthest from him which did not seem familiar. It was in blue letters on a yellow ground, and all that he could read of it was a name—John Harrington—and something like a date.

It could be of no interest to him to know more; but for all that, as the car emptied, he was just curious enough to move along the seat until he could read it well. He felt to a slight extent repaid for his trouble; the advertisement was not of the usual type. It ran thus: "In memory of John Harrington, F.S.A., of The Laurels, Ashbrooke. Died Sept. 18th, 1889. Three months were allowed."

The car stopped. Mr Dunning, still contemplating the blue letters on the yellow ground, had to be stimulated to rise by a word from the conductor. "I beg your pardon," he said, "I was looking at that advertisement; it's a very odd one, isn't it?" The conductor read it slowly. "Well, my word," he said, "I never see that one before. Well, that is a cure, ain't it? Someone bin up to their jokes 'ere, I should think." He got out a duster and applied it, not without saliva, to the pane and then to the outside. "No," he said, returning, "that ain't no transfer; seems to me as if it was reg'lar *in* the glass, what I mean in the substance, as you may say. Don't you think so, sir?" Mr Dunning examined it and rubbed it with his glove, and agreed. "Who looks after these advertisements, and gives leave for them to be put up? I wish you would inquire. I will just take a note of the words." At this moment there came a call from the driver, "Look alive, George, time's up." "All right, all right; there's somethink else what's up at this end. You come and look at this 'ere glass." "What's gorn with the glass?" said the driver, approaching. "Well, and oo's 'Arrington? What's it all about?" "I was just asking who was responsible for putting the advertisements up in your cars, and saying it would be as well to make some inquiry about this one." "Well, sir, that's all done at the Company's orfice, that work is: it's our Mr Timms, I believe, looks into that. When we put up tonight I'll leave word, and per'aps I'll be able to tell you tomorrer if you 'appen to be coming this way."

This was all that passed that evening. Mr Dunning did just go to the trouble of looking up Ashbrooke, and found that it was in Warwickshire.

Next day he went to town again. The car (it was the same car) was too full in the morning to allow of his getting a word with the conductor: he could only be sure that the curious advertisement had been made away with. The close of the day brought a further element of mystery into the transaction. He had missed the tram, or else preferred walking home, but at a rather late hour, while he was at work in his study, one of the maids came to say that two men from the tramways was very anxious to speak to him. This was a reminder of the advertisement, which he had, he says, nearly forgotten. He had the men in—they were the conductor and driver of the car—and when the matter of refreshment had been attended to, asked what Mr Timms had had to say about the advertisement. "Well, sir, that's what we took the liberty to step round about," said the conductor. "Mr Timm's 'e give William 'ere the rough side of his tongue about that: 'cordin' to 'im there warn't no advertisement of that description sent in, nor ordered, nor paid for, nor put up, nor nothink, let alone not bein' there, and we was playing the fool takin' up his time. 'Well,' I says, 'if that's the case, all I ask of you, Mr Timms,' I says, 'is to take and look at it for yourself,' I says. 'Of course if it ain't there,' I says, 'you may take and call me what you like.' 'Right,' he says, 'I will': and we went straight off. Now, I leave it to you, sir, if that ad., as we term 'em, with 'Arrington on it warn't as plain as ever you see anythink—blue letters on yeller glass, and as I says at the time, and you borne me out, reg'lar *in* the glass, because, if you remember, you recollect of me swabbing it with my duster." "To be sure I do, quite clearly—well?" "You may say well, I don't think. Mr Timms he gets in that car with a light—no, he telled William to 'old the light outside. 'Now,' he says, 'where's your precious ad. what we've 'eard so much about?' ''Ere it is,' I says, 'Mr Timms,' and I laid my 'and on it." The conductor paused.

"Well," said Mr Dunning, "it was gone, I suppose. Broken?"

"Broke!—not it. There warn't, if you'll believe me, no more trace of them letters—blue letters they was—on that piece o' glass, than—well, it's no good *me* talkin'. I never see such a thing. I leave it to William here if—but there, as I says, where's the benefit in me going on about it?"

"And what did Mr Timms say?"

"Why 'e did what I give 'im leave to—called us pretty much anythink he liked, and I don't know as I blame him so much neither. But what we thought, William and me did, was as we seen you take down a bit of a note about that—well, that letterin'——"

"I certainly did that, and I have it now. Did you wish me to speak to Mr Timms myself, and show it to him? Was that what you came in about?"

"There, didn't I say as much?" said William. "Deal with a gent if you can get on the track of one, that's my word. Now perhaps, George, you'll allow as I ain't took you very far wrong tonight."

"Very well, William, very well; no need for you to go on as if you'd 'ad to frog's-march me 'ere. I come quiet, didn't I? All the same for that, we 'adn't ought to take up your time this way, sir; but if it so 'appened you could find time to step round to the Company's orfice in the morning and tell Mr Timms what you seen for yourself, we should lay under a very 'igh obligation to you for the trouble. You see it ain't bein' called—well, one thing and another, as we mind, but if they got it into their 'ead at the orfice as we seen things as warn't there, why, one thing leads to another, and where we should be a twelvemunce 'ence—well, you can understand what I mean."

Amid further elucidations of the proposition, George, conducted by William, left the room.

The incredulity of Mr Timms (who had a nodding acquaintance with Mr Dunning) was greatly modified on the following day by what the latter could tell and show him; and any bad mark that might have been attached to the names of

77

William and George was not suffered to remain on the Company's books; but explanation there was none.

Mr Dunning's interest in the matter was kept alive by an incident of the following afternoon. He was walking from his club to the train, and he noticed some way ahead a man with a handful of leaflets such as are distributed to passers-by by agents of enterprising firms. This agent had not chosen a very crowded street for his operations: in fact, Mr Dunning did not see him get rid of a single leaflet before he himself reached the spot. One was thrust into his hand as he passed: the hand that gave it touched his, and he experienced a sort of little shock as it did so. It seemed unnaturally rough and hot. He looked in passing at the giver, but the impression he got was so unclear that, however much he tried to reckon it up subsequently, nothing would come. He was walking quickly, and as he went on glanced at the paper. It was a blue one. The name of Harrington in large capitals caught his eye. He stopped, startled, and felt for his glasses. The next instant the leaflet was twitched out of his hand by a man who hurried past, and was irrecoverably gone. He ran back a few paces, but where was the passer-by? and where the distributor?

It was in a somewhat pensive frame of mind that Mr Dunning passed on the following day into the Select Manuscript Room of the British Museum, and filled up tickets for Harley 3586, and some other volumes. After a few minutes they were brought to him, and he was settling the one he wanted first upon the desk, when he thought he heard his own name whispered behind him. He turned round hastily, and in doing so, brushed his little portfolio of loose papers on to the floor. He saw no one he recognized except one of the staff in charge of the room, who nodded to him, and he proceeded to pick up his papers. He thought he had them all, and was turning to begin work, when a stout gentleman at the table behind him, who was just rising to leave, and had collected his own belongings, touched him on the shoulder, saying, "May I give you this? I think it should be yours," and handed him a missing quire. "It is mine, thank you," said Mr Dunning. In another moment the man had left the room. Upon finishing his work for the afternoon, Mr Dunning had some conversation with the assistant in charge, and took occasion to ask who the stout gentleman was. "Oh, he's a man named Karswell," said the assistant; "he was asking me a week ago who were the great authorities on alchemy, and of course I told him you were the only one in the country. I'll see if I can't catch him: he'd like to meet you, I'm sure."

"For heaven's sake don't dream of it!" said Mr Dunning, "I'm particularly anxious to avoid him."

"Oh! very well," said the assistant, "he doesn't come here often: I dare say you won't meet him."

More than once on the way home that day Mr Dunning confessed to himself that he did not look forward with his usual cheerfulness to a solitary evening. It seemed to him that something ill-defined and impalpable had stepped in between him and his fellow-men—had taken him in charge, as it were. He wanted to sit close up to his neighbours in the train and in the tram, but as luck would have it both train and car were markedly empty. The conductor George was thoughtful, and appeared to be absorbed in calculations as to the number of passengers. On arriving at his house he found Dr Watson, his medical man, on his doorstep. "I've had to upset your household arrangements, I'm sorry to say, Dunning. Both your servants *hors de combat*. In fact, I've had to send them to the Nursing Home."

"Good heavens! what's the matter?"

"It's something like ptomaine poisoning, I should think: you've not suffered yourself, I can see, or you wouldn't be walking about. I think they'll pull through all right."

"Dear, dear! Have you any idea what brought it on?"

"Well, they tell me they bought some shell-fish from a hawker at their dinner-time. It's odd. I've made inquiries, but I can't find that any hawker has been to other houses in the street. I couldn't send word to you; they won't be back for a bit yet. You come and dine with me tonight, anyhow, and we can make arrangements for going on. Eight o'clock. Don't be too anxious."

The solitary evening was thus obviated; at the expense of some distress and inconvenience, it is true. Mr Dunning spent the time pleasantly enough with the doctor (a rather recent settler), and returned to his lonely home at about 11.30. The night he passed is not one on which he looks back with any satisfaction. He was in bed and the light was out. He was wondering if the charwoman would come early enough to get him hot water next morning, when he heard the unmistakable sound of his study door opening. No step followed it on the passage floor, but the sound must mean mischief, for he knew that he had shut the door that evening after putting his papers away in his desk. It was rather shame than courage that induced him to slip out into the passage and lean over the banister in his nightgown, listening. No light was visible; no further sound came: only a gust of warm, or even hot air played for an instant round his shins. He went back and decided to lock himself into his room. There was more unpleasantness, however. Either an economical suburban company had decided that their light would not be required in the small hours, and had stopped working, or else something was wrong with the meter; the effect was in any case that the electric light was off. The obvious course was to find a match, and also to consult his watch: he might as well know how many hours of discomfort awaited him. So he put his hand into the well-known nook under the pillow: only, it did not get so far. What he touched was, according to his account, a mouth, with teeth, and with hair about it, and, he declares, not the mouth of a human being. I do not think it is any use to guess what he said or did; but he was in a spare room with the door locked and his ear to it before he was clearly conscious again. And there he spent the rest of a most miserable night, looking every moment for some fumbling at the door: but nothing came.

The venturing back to his own room in the morning was attended with many listenings and quiverings. The door stood open, fortunately, and the blinds were up (the servants had been out of the house before the hour of drawing them down); there was, to be short, no trace of an inhabitant. The watch, too, was in its usual place; nothing was disturbed, only the wardrobe door had swung open, in accordance with its confirmed habit. A ring at the back door now announced the charwoman, who had been ordered the night before, and nerved Mr Dunning, after letting her in, to continue his search in other parts of the house. It was equally fruitless.

The day thus begun went on dismally enough. He dared not go to the Museum: in spite of what the assistant had said, Karswell might turn up there, and Dunning felt he could not cope with a probably hostile stranger. His own house was odious; he hated sponging on the doctor. He spent some little time in a call at the Nursing Home, where he was slightly cheered by a good report of his housekeeper and maid. Towards lunch-time he betook himself to his club, again experiencing a gleam of satisfaction at seeing the Secretary of the Association. At luncheon Dunning told his friend the more material of his woes, but could not bring himself to speak of those that weighed most heavily on his spirits. "My poor dear man," said the Secretary, "what an upset! Look here: we're alone at home, absolutely. You must put up with us. Yes! no excuse: send your things in this afternoon." Dunning was unable to stand out: he was, in truth, becoming acutely anxious, as the hours went on, as to what that night might have waiting for him. He was almost happy as he hurried home to pack up.

His friends, when they had time to take stock of him, were rather shocked at his lorn appearance, and did their best to keep him up to the mark. Not altogether without success: but, when the two men were smoking alone later, Dunning became dull again. Suddenly he said, "Gayton, I believe that alchemist man knows it was I who got his paper rejected."

Gayton whistled. "What makes you think that?" he said. Dunning told of his conversation with the Museum assistant, and Gayton could only agree that the guess seemed likely to be correct. "Not that I care much," Dunning went on, "only it might be a nuisance if we were to meet. He's a bad-tempered party, I imagine." Conversation dropped again; Gayton became more and more strongly impressed with the desolateness that came over Dunning's face and bearing, and finally—though with a considerable effort—he asked him point-blank whether something serious was not bothering him. Dunning gave an exclamation of relief. "I was perishing to get it off my mind," he said. "Do you know anything about a man named John Harrington?" Gayton was thoroughly startled, and at the moment could only ask why. Then the complete story of Dunning's experiences came out—what had happened in the tramcar, in his own house, and in the street, the troubling of spirit that had crept over him, and still held him; and he ended with the question he had begun with. Gayton was at a loss how to answer him. To tell the story of Harrington's end would perhaps be right; only, Dunning was in a nervous state, the story was a grim one, and he could not help asking himself whether there were not a connecting link between these two cases, in the person of Karswell. It was a difficult concession for a scientific man, but it could be eased by the phrase "hypnotic suggestion". In the end he decided that his answer tonight should be guarded; he would talk the situation over with his wife. So he said that he had known Harrington at Cambridge, and believed he had died suddenly in 1889, adding a few details about the man and his published work. He did talk over the matter with Mrs Gayton, and, as he had anticipated, she leapt at once to the conclusion which had been hovering before him. It was she who reminded him of the surviving brother, Henry Harrington, and she also who suggested that he might be got hold of by means of their hosts of the day before. "He might be a hopeless crank," objected Gayton. "That could be ascertained from the Bennetts, who knew him," Mrs Gayton retorted; and she undertook to see the Bennetts the very next day.

It is not necessary to tell in further detail the steps by which Henry Harrington and Dunning were brought together.

The next scene that does require to be narrated is a conversation that took place between the two. Dunning had told Harrington of the strange ways in which the dead man's name had been brought before him, and had said something, besides, of his own subsequent experiences. Then he had asked if Harrington was disposed, in return, to recall any of the circumstances connected with his brother's death. Harrington's surprise at what he heard can be imagined: but his reply was readily given.

"John," he said, "was in a very odd state, undeniably, from time to time, during some weeks before, though not immediately before, the catastrophe. There were several things; the principal notion he had was that he thought he was being followed. No doubt he was an impressionable man, but he never had had such fancies as this before. I cannot get it out of my mind that there was ill-will at work, and what you tell me about yourself reminds me very much of my brother. Can you think of any possible connecting link?"

"There is just one that has been taking shape vaguely in my mind. I've been told that your brother reviewed a book very severely not long before he died, and just lately I have happened to cross the path of the man who wrote that book in a way he would resent."

"Don't tell me the man was called Karswell."

"Why not? that is exactly his name."

Henry Harrington leant back. "That is final to my mind. Now I must explain further. From something he said, I feel sure that my brother John was beginning to believe—very much against his will—that Karswell was at the bottom of his trouble. I want to tell you what seems to me to have a bearing on the situation. My brother was a great musician, and used to run up to concerts in town. He came back, three months before he died, from one of these, and gave me his programme to look at—an analytical programme: he always kept them. 'I nearly missed this one,' he said. 'I suppose I must have dropped it: anyhow, I was looking for it under my seat and in my pockets and so on, and my neighbour offered me his: said "might he give it me, he had no further use for it," and he went away just afterwards. I don't know who he was—a stout, clean-shaven man. I should have been sorry to miss it; of course I could have bought another, but this cost me nothing.' At another time he told me that he had been very uncomfortable both on the way to his hotel and during the night. I piece things together now in thinking it over. Then, not very long after, he was going over these programmes, putting them in order to have them bound up, and in this particular one (which by the way I had hardly glanced at), he found quite near the beginning a strip of paper with some very odd writing on it in red and black—most carefully done—it looked to me more like Runic letters than anything else. 'Why,' he said, 'this must belong to my fat neighbour. It looks as if it might be worth returning to him; it may be a copy of something; evidently someone had taken trouble over it. How can I find his address?' We talked it over for a little and agreed that it wasn't worth advertising about, and that my brother had better look out for the man at the next concert, to which he was going very soon. The paper was lying on the book and we were both by the fire; it was a cold, windy summer evening. I suppose the door blew open, though I didn't notice it: at any rate a gust—a warm gust it was—came quite suddenly between us, took the paper and blew it straight into the fire: it was light, thin paper, and flared and went up the chimney in a single ash. 'Well,' I said, 'you can't give it back now.' He said nothing for a minute: then rather crossly, 'No, I can't; but why you should keep on saying so I don't know.' I remarked that I didn't say it more than once. 'Not more than four times, you mean,' was all he said. I remember all that very clearly, without any good reason; and now to come to the point. I don't know if you looked at that book of Karswell's which my unfortunate brother reviewed. It's not likely that you should: but I did, both before his death and after it. The first time we made game of it together. It was written in no style at all—split infinitives, and every sort of thing that makes an Oxford gorge rise. Then there was nothing that the man didn't swallow: mixing up classical myths, and stories out of the *Golden Legend* with reports of savage customs of today—all very proper, no doubt, if you know how to use them, but he didn't: he seemed to put the *Golden Legend* and the *Golden Bough* exactly on a par, and to believe both: a pitiable exhibition, in short. Well, after the misfortune, I looked over the book again. It was no better than before, but the impression which it left this time on my mind was different. I suspected—as I told you—that Karswell had borne ill-will to my brother, even that he was in some way responsible for what had happened; and now his book seemed to me to be a very sinister performance indeed. One chapter in particular struck me, in which he spoke of 'casting the Runes' on people, either for the purpose of gaining their affection or of getting them out of the way—perhaps more especially the latter: he spoke of all this in a way that really seemed to me to imply actual knowledge. I've not time to go into details, but the upshot is that I am pretty sure from information received that the civil man at the concert was Karswell: I suspect—I more than suspect—that the paper was of importance: and I do believe that if my brother had been able to give it back, he might have been alive now. Therefore, it occurs to me to ask you whether you have anything to put beside what I have told you."

By way of answer, Dunning had the episode in the Manuscript Room at the British Museum to relate. "Then he did actually hand you some papers; have you examined them?

No? because we must, if you'll allow it, look at them at once, and very carefully."

They went to the still empty house—empty, for the two servants were not yet able to return to work. Dunning's portfolio of papers was gathering dust on the writing-table. In it were the quires of small-sized scribbling paper which he used for his transcripts: and from one of these, as he took it up, there slipped and fluttered out into the room with un-canny quickness, a strip of thin light paper. The window was open, but Harrington slammed it to, just in time to inter-cept the paper, which he caught. "I thought so," he said; "it might be the identical thing that was given to my brother. You'll have to look out, Dunning; this may mean something quite serious for you."

A long consultation took place. The paper was narrowly examined. As Harrington had said, the characters on it were more like Runes than anything else, but not decipherable by either man, and both hesitated to copy them, for fear, as they confessed, of perpetuating whatever evil purpose they might conceal. So it has remained impossible (if I may anticipate a little) to ascertain what was conveyed in this curious message or commission. Both Dunning and Harrington are firmly convinced that it had the effect of bringing its possessors into very undesirable company. That it must be returned to the source whence it came they were agreed, and further, that the only safe and certain way was that of personal service; and here contrivance would be necessary, for Dunning was known by sight to Karswell. He must, for one thing, alter his appearance by shaving his beard. But then might not the blow fall first? Harrington thought they could time it. He knew the date of the concert at which the "black spot" had been put on his brother: it was June 18th. The death had followed on Sept. 18th. Dunning reminded him that three months had been mentioned on the inscription on the car-window. "Perhaps," he added, with a cheerless laugh, "mine may be a bill at three months too. I believe I can fix it by my diary. Yes, April 23rd was the day at the Museum; that brings us to July 23rd. Now, you know, it becomes extremely important to me to know anything you will tell me about the progress of your brother's trouble, if it is possible for you to speak of it." "Of course. Well, the sense of being watched whenever he was alone was the most distressing thing to him. After a time I took to sleeping in his room, and he was the better for that: still, he talked a great deal in his sleep. What about? Is it wise to dwell on that, at least before things are straightened out? I think not, but I can tell you this: two things came for him by post during those weeks, both with a London postmark, and addressed in a commercial hand. One was a woodcut of Bewick's, roughly torn out of the page: one which shows a moonlit road and a man walking along it, followed by an awful demon creature. Under it were written the lines out of the 'Ancient Mariner' (which I suppose the cut illustrates) about one who, having once looked round—

> 'walks on,
> And turns no more his head,
> Because he knows a frightful fiend
> Doth close behind him tread.'

The other was a calendar, such as tradesmen often send. My brother paid no attention to this, but I looked at it after his death, and found that everything after Sept. 18 had been torn out. You may be surprised at his having gone out alone the evening he was killed, but the fact is that during the last ten days or so of his life he had been quite free from the sense of being followed or watched."

The end of the consultation was this. Harrington, who knew a neighbour of Karswell's, thought he saw a way of keeping a watch on his movements. It would be Dunning's part to be in readiness to try to cross Karswell's path at any moment, to keep the paper safe and in a place of ready access.

They parted. The next weeks were no doubt a severe strain upon Dunning's nerves: the intangible barrier which had seemed to rise about him on the day when he received the paper, gradually developed into a brooding blackness that cut him off from the means of escape to which one might have thought he might resort. No one was at hand who was likely to suggest them to him, and he seemed robbed of all initiative. He waited with inexpressible anxiety as May, June, and early July passed on, for a mandate from Harrington. But all this time Karswell remained immovable at Lufford.

At last, in less than a week before the date he had come to look upon as the end of his earthly activities, came a telegram, "Leaves Victoria by boat train Thursday night. Do not miss. I come to you tonight. Harrington."

He arrived accordingly, and they concocted plans. The train left Victoria at nine and its last stop before Dover was Croydon West. Harrington would mark down Karswell at Victoria, and look out for Dunning at Croydon, calling to him if need were by a name agreed upon. Dunning, disguised as far as might be, was to have no label or initials on any hand luggage, and must at all costs have the paper with him.

Dunning's suspense as he waited on the Croydon platform I need not attempt to describe. His sense of danger during the last days had only been sharpened by the fact that the cloud about him had perceptibly been lighter; but relief was an ominous symptom, and, if Karswell eluded him now, hope was gone: and there were so many chances of that. The rumour of the journey might be itself a device. The twenty minutes in which he paced the platform and persecuted every porter with inquiries as to the boat train were as bitter as any he had spent. Still, the train came, and Harrington was at the window. It was important, of course, that there should be no recognition: so Dunning got in at the farther end of the corridor carriage, and only gradually made his way to the compartment where Harrington and Karswell were. He was pleased, on the whole, to see that the train was far from full.

Karswell was on the alert, but gave no sign of recognition. Dunning took the seat not immediately facing him, and attempted, vainly at first, then with increasing command of his faculties, to reckon the possibilities of making the desired transfer. Opposite to Karswell, and next to Dunning, was a heap of Karswell's coats on the seat. It would be of no use to slip the paper into these—he would not be safe, or would not feel so, unless in some way it could be proffered by him and accepted by the other. There was a handbag, open, and with papers in it. Could he manage to conceal this (so that perhaps Karswell might leave the carriage without it), and then find and give it to him? This was the plan that suggested itself. If he could only have counselled with Harrington! but that could not be. The minutes went on. More than once Karswell rose and went out into the corridor. The second time Dunning was on the point of attempting to make the bag fall off the seat, but he caught Harrington's eye, and read in it a warning. Karswell, from the corridor, was watching: probably to see if the two men recognized each other. He returned, but was evidently restless: and, when he rose the third time, hope dawned, for something did slip off his seat and fall with hardly a sound to the floor. Karswell went out once more, and passed out of range of the corridor window. Dunning picked up what had fallen, and saw that the key was in his hands in the form of one of Cook's ticket-cases, with tickets in it. These cases have a pocket in the cover, and within very few seconds the paper of which we have heard was in the pocket of this one. To make the operation more secure, Harrington stood in the doorway of the compartment and fiddled with the blind. It was done, and done at the right time, for the train was now slowing down towards Dover.

In a moment more Karswell re-entered the compartment. As he did so, Dunning, managing, he knew not how, to suppress the tremble in his voice, handed him the ticket-case, saying, "May I give you this, sir? I believe it is yours." After a brief glance at the ticket inside, Karswell uttered the hoped-for response, "Yes, it is; much obliged to you, sir," and he placed it in his breast pocket.

LIFE IN ACTION

Even in the few moments that remained—moments of tense anxiety, for they knew not to what a premature finding of the paper might lead—both men noticed that the carriage seemed to darken about them and to grow warmer; that Karswell was fidgety and oppressed; that he drew the heap of loose coats near to him and cast it back as if it repelled him; and that he then sat upright and glanced anxiously at both. They, with sickening anxiety, busied themselves in collecting their belongings; but they both thought that Karswell was on the point of speaking when the train stopped at Dover Town. It was natural that in the short space between town and pier they should both go into the corridor.

At the pier they got out, but so empty was the train that they were forced to linger on the platform until Karswell should have passed ahead of them with his porter on the way to the boat, and only then was it safe for them to exchange a pressure of the hand and a word of concentrated congratulation. The effect upon Dunning was to make him almost faint. Harrington made him lean up against the wall, while he himself went forward a few yards within sight of the gangway to the boat, at which Karswell had now arrived. The man at the head of it examined his ticket, and, laden with coats, he passed down into the boat. Suddenly the official called after him, "You, sir, beg pardon, did the other gentleman show his ticket?" "What the devil do you mean by the other gentleman?" Karswell's snarling voice called back from the deck. The man bent over and looked at him. "The devil? Well, I don't know, I'm sure," Harrington heard him say to himself, and then aloud, "My mistake, sir; must have been your rugs! ask your pardon." And then, to a subordinate near him, "'Ad he got a dog with him, or what? Funny thing: I could 'a' swore 'e wasn't alone. Well, whatever it was, they'll 'ave to see to it aboard. She's off now. Another week and we shall be gettin' the 'oliday customers." In five minutes more there was nothing but the lessening lights of the boat, the long line of the Dover lamps, the night breeze, and the moon.

Long and long the two sat in their room at the Lord Warden. In spite of the removal of their greatest anxiety, they were oppressed with a doubt, not of the lightest. Had they been justified in sending a man to his death, as they believed they had? Ought they not to warn him, at least? "No," said Harrington; "if he is the murderer I think him, we have done no more than is just. Still, if you think it better—but how and where can you warn him?" "He was booked to Abbeville only," said Dunning. "I saw that. If I wired to the hotels there in Joanne's Guide, 'Examine your ticket-case, Dunning,' I should feel happier. This is the 21st: he will have a day. But I am afraid he has gone into the dark." So telegrams were left at the hotel office.

It is not clear whether these reached their destination, or whether, if they did, they were understood. All that is known is that, on the afternoon of the 23rd, an English traveller, examining the front of St Wulfram's Church at Abbeville, then under extensive repair, was struck on the head and instantly killed by a stone falling from the scaffold erected round the north-western tower, there being, as was clearly proved, no workman on the scaffold at that moment: and the traveller's papers identified him as Mr Karswell.

Only one detail shall be added. At Karswell's sale a set of Bewick, sold with all faults, was acquired by Harrington. The page with the woodcut of the traveller and the demon was, as he had expected, mutilated. Also, after a judicious interval, Harrington repeated to Dunning something of what he had heard his brother say in his sleep: but it was not long before Dunning stopped him.

The Enemy

V. S. NAIPAUL

I HAD always considered this woman, my mother, as the enemy. She was sure to misunderstand anything I did, and the time came when I thought she not only misunderstood me, but quite definitely disapproved of me. I was an only child, but for her I was one too many.

She hated my father, and even after he died she continued to hate him.

She would say, "Go ahead and do what you doing. You is your father child, you hear, not mine."

The real split between my mother and me happened not in Miguel Street, but in the country.

My mother had decided to leave my father, and she wanted to take me to her mother.

I refused to go.

My father was ill, and in bed. Besides, he had promised that if I stayed with him I was to have a whole box of crayons.

I chose the crayons and my father.

We were living at the time in Cunupia, where my father was a driver on the sugar estates. He wasn't a slave-driver, but a driver of free people, but my father used to behave as though the people were slaves. He rode about the estates on a big clumsy brown horse, cracking his whip at the labourers and people said—I really don't believe this—that he used to kick the labourers.

I don't believe it because my father had lived all his life in Cunupia, and he knew that you really couldn't push the Cunupia people around. They are not tough people, but they think nothing of killing, and they are prepared to wait years for the chance to kill someone they don't like. In fact, Cunupia and Tableland are the two parts of Trinidad where murders occur often enough to ensure quick promotion for the policemen stationed there.

At first we lived in the barracks, but then my father wanted to move to a little wooden house not far away.

My mother said, "You playing hero. Go and live in your house by yourself, you hear."

She was afraid, of course, but my father insisted. So we moved to the house, and then trouble really started.

A man came to the house one day about midday and said to my mother, "Where your husband?"

My mother said, "I don't know."

The man was cleaning his teeth with a twig from a hibiscus plant. He spat and said, "It don't matter. I have time. I could wait."

My mother said, "You ain't doing nothing like that. I know what you thinking, but I have my sister coming here right now."

The man laughed and said, "I not doing anything. I just want to know when he coming home."

I began to cry in terror.

The man laughed.

My mother said, "Shut up this minute or I give you something really to cry about."

I went to another room and walked about saying, "Rama! Rama! Sita Rama!" This was what my father had told me to say when I was in danger of any sort.

I looked out of the window. It was bright daylight, and hot, and there was nobody else in all the wide world of bush and trees.

And then I saw my aunt walking up the road.

She came and she said, "Anything wrong with you here? I was at home just sitting quite quiet, and I suddenly feel that something was going wrong. I feel I had to come to see."

The man said, "Yes, I know the feeling."

My mother, who was being very brave all the time, began to cry.

But all this was only to frighten us, and we were certainly frightened. My father always afterwards took his gun with him, and my mother kept a sharpened cutlass by her hand.

Then, at night, there used to be voices, sometimes from the road, sometimes from the bushes behind the house. The voices came from people who had lost their way and wanted lights, people who had come to tell my father that his sister had died suddenly in Debe, people who had come just to tell my father that there was a big fire at the sugar-mill. Sometimes there would be two or three of these voices, speaking from different directions, and we would sit awake in the dark house, just waiting, waiting for the voices to fall silent. And when they did fall silent it was even more terrible.

My father used to say, "They still outside. They want you to go out and look."

And at four or five o'clock when the morning light was coming up we would hear the tramp of feet in the bush, feet going away.

As soon as darkness fell we would lock ourselves up in the house, and wait. For days there would sometimes be nothing at all, and then we would hear them again.

My father brought home a dog one day. We called it Tarzan. He was more of a playful dog than a watch-dog, a big hairy brown dog, and I would ride on its back.

When evening came I said, "Tarzan coming in with us?"

He wasn't. He remained whining outside the door, scratching it with his paws.

Tarzan didn't last long.

One morning we found him hacked to pieces and flung on the top step.

We hadn't heard any noise the night before.

My mother began to quarrel with my father, but my father was behaving as though he didn't really care what happened to him or to any of us.

My mother used to say, "You playing brave. But bravery ain't going to give any of us life, you hear. Let us leave this place."

My father began hanging up words of hope on the walls of the house, things from the Gita and the Bible, and sometimes things he just made up.

He also lost his temper more often with my mother, and the time came when as soon as she entered a room he would scream and pelt things at her.

So she went back to her mother, and I remained with my father.

During those days my father spent a lot of his time in bed, and so I had to lie down with him. For the first time I really talked to my father. He taught me three things.

The first was this.

"Boy," my father asked, "Who is your father?"

I said, "You is my father."

"Wrong."

"How that wrong?"

My father said, "You want to know who your father really is? God is your father."

"And what you is, then?"

"Me, what I is? I is—let me see, well, I is just a second sort of father, not your real father."

This teaching was later to get me into trouble, particularly with my mother.

The second thing my father taught me was the law of gravity.

We were sitting on the edge of the bed, and he dropped the box of matches.

He asked, "Now, boy, tell me why the matches drop."

I said, "But they bound to drop. What you want them to do? Go sideways?"

My father said, "I will tell why they drop. They drop because of the laws of gravity."

And he showed me a trick. He half filled a bucket with water and spun the bucket fast over his shoulder.

He said, "Look, the water wouldn't fall."

But it did. He got a soaking and the floor was wet.

He said, "It don't matter. I just put too much water, that's all. Look again."

The second time it worked.

The third thing my father taught me was the blending of colours. This was just a few days before he died. He was very ill, and he used to spend a lot of time shivering and mumbling; and even when he fell asleep I used to hear him groaning.

I remained with him on the bed most of the time.

He said to me one day, "You got the coloured pencils?"

I took them from under the pillow.

He said, "You want to see some magic?"

I said, "What, you know magic really?"

He took the yellow pencil and filled in a yellow square.

He asked, "Boy, what colour this is?"

I said, "Yellow."

He said, "Just pass me the blue pencil now, and shut your eyes tight tight."

When I opened my eyes he said, "Boy, what colour this square is now?"

I said, "You sure you ain't cheating?"

He laughed and showed me how blue and yellow make green.

I said, "You mean if I take a leaf and wash it and wash it and wash it really good, it go be yellow or blue when I finish with it?"

He said, "No. You see, is God who blend those colours. God, your father."

I spent a lot of my time trying to make up tricks. The only one I could do was to put two match-heads together, light them, and make them stick. But my father knew that. But at last I found a trick that I was sure my father didn't know. He never got to know about it because he died on the night I was to show it him.

It had been a day of great heat, and in the afternoon the sky had grown low and heavy and black. It felt almost chilly in the house, and my father was sitting wrapped up in the rocking chair. The rain began to fall drop by heavy drop, beating like a hundred fists on the roof. It grew dark, and I lit the oil lamp, sticking in a pin in the wick, to keep away bad spirits from the house.

My father suddenly stopped rocking and whispered, "Boy, they here tonight. Listen. Listen."

We were both silent and I listened carefully, but my ears could catch nothing but the wind and the rain.

A window banged itself open. The wind whooshed in with heavy raindrops.

"God!" my father screamed.

I went to the window. It was a pitch-black night, and the world was a wild and lonely place, with only the wind and the rain on the leaves. I had to fight to pull the window in, and before I could close it, I saw the sky light up with a crack of lightning.

I shut the window and waited for the thunder.

It sounded like a steam-roller on the roof.

My father said, "Boy, don't frighten. Say what I tell you to say."

I went and sat at the foot of the rocking chair and I began to say, "Rama! Rama! Sita Rama!"

My father joined in. He was shivering with cold and fright.

Suddenly he shouted, "Boy, they here. They here. I hear them talking under the house. They could do what they like in all this noise, and nobody could hear them."

I said, "Don't be fraid, I have this cutlass here, and you have your gun."

But my father wasn't listening.

He said, "But it dark, man. It so dark. It so dark."

I got up and went to the table for the oil lamp to bring it nearer. But just then there was an explosion of thunder so low it might have been just above the roof. It rolled and rumbled for a long long time. Then another window blew open and the oil lamp was blown out. The wind and the rain tore into the dark room.

My father screamed out once more, "Oh God, it dark."

I was lost in a black world. I screamed until the thunder died away and the rain had become a drizzle. I forgot all about the trick I had prepared for my father: the soap I had rubbed into the palms of my hands until it had dried and disappeared.

Everybody agreed on one thing. My mother and I had to leave the country. Port-of-Spain was the safest place. There was, too, a lot of laughter against my father, and it appeared that for the rest of my life I would have to bear the cross of a father who died from fright. But in a month or so I had forgotten my father, and I had begun to look upon myself as the boy who had no father. It seemed natural.

In fact, when we moved to Port-of-Spain and I saw what the normal relationship between father and son was—it was nothing more than the relationship between the beater and the beaten—when I saw this I was grateful.

My mother made a great thing at first about keeping me in my place and knocking out all the nonsense my father had taught me. I don't know why she didn't try harder, but the fact is that she soon lost interest in me, and she let me run about the street, only rushing down to beat me from time to time.

Occasionally, though, she would take the old firm line.

One day she kept me home. She said, "No school for you today. I just sick of tying your shoe-laces for you. Today you go have to learn that!"

I didn't think she was being fair. After all, in the country none of us wore shoes, and I wasn't used to them.

That day she beat me and beat me and made me tie knot after knot, and in the end I still couldn't tie my shoelaces. For years afterwards it was a great shame to me that I couldn't do a simple thing like that, just as how I couldn't peel an orange. But about the shoes I made up a little trick. I never made my mother buy shoes the correct size. I pretended that those shoes hurt, and I made her get me shoes a size or two bigger. Once the attendant had tied the laces up for me, I never undid them, and I merely slipped my feet in and out of the shoes. To keep them on my feet, I stuck paper in the toes.

To hear my mother talk, you would think I was a freak. Nearly every little boy she knew was better and more intelligent. There was one boy she knew who helped his mother paint her house. There was another boy who could mend his own shoes. There was still another boy who at the age of thirteen was earning a good twenty dollars a month, while I was just idling and living off her blood.

Still, there were surprising glimpses of kindness.

There was the time, for instance, when I was cleaning some tumblers for her one Saturday morning. I dropped a tumbler and it broke. Before I could do anything about it my mother saw what had happened.

She said, "How you break it?"

I said, "It just slip off. It smooth smooth."

She said, "Is a lot of nonsense drinking from glass. They break up so easy."

And that was all. I got worried about my mother's health. She was never worried about mine.

She thought that there was no illness in the world a stiff dose of hot Epsom Salts couldn't cure. That was a penance I had to endure once a month. It completely ruined my weekend. And if there was something she couldn't understand, she sent me to the Health Office in Tragarete Road. That was an awful place. You waited and waited and waited before you went in to see the doctor.

Before you had time to say, "Doctor, I have a pain—" he

99

would be writing out a prescription for you. And again you had to wait for the medicine. All the Health Office medicines were the same. Water and a pink sediment half an inch thick.

Hat used to say of the Health Office, "The Government take up faith healing."

My mother considered the Health Office a good place for me to go to. I would go there at eight in morning and return any time after two in the afternoon. It kept me out of mischief, and it cost only twenty-four cents a year.

But you mustn't get the impression that I was a saint all the time. I wasn't. I used to have odd fits where I just couldn't take an order from anybody, particularly my mother. I used to feel that I would dishonour myself for life if I took anybody's orders. And life is a funny thing, really. I sometimes got these fits just when my mother was anxious to be nice to me.

The day after Hat rescued me from drowning at Dockside I wrote an essay for my schoolmaster on the subject, "A Day at the Seaside". I don't think any schoolmaster ever got an essay like that. I talked about how I was nearly drowned and how calmly I was facing death, with my mind absolutely calm, thinking, "Well, boy, this is the end." The teacher was so pleased he gave me ten marks out of twelve.

He said, "I think you are a genius."

When I went home I told my mother, "That essay I write today, I get ten out of twelve for it."

My mother said, "How you so bold-face to lie brave brave so in front of my face? You want me give you a slap to turn your face?"

In the end I convinced her.

She melted at once. She sat down in the hammock and said, "Come and sit down by me, son."

Just then the crazy fit came on me.

I got very angry for no reason at all and I said, "No, I not going to sit by you."

She laughed and coaxed.

And the angrier she made me.

Slowly the friendliness died away. It had become a struggle between two wills. I was prepared to drown rather than dishonour myself by obeying.

"I ask you to come and sit down here."

"I not sitting down."

"Take off your belt."

I took it off and gave it to her. She belted me soundly, and my nose bled, but still I didn't sit in the hammock.

At times like these I used to cry, without meaning it, "If my father was alive you wouldn't be behaving like this."

So she remained the enemy. She was someone from whom I was going to escape as soon as I grew big enough. That was, in fact, the main lure of adulthood.

Progress was sweeping through Port-of-Spain in those days. The Americans were pouring money into Trinidad and there was a lot of talk from the British about colonial development and welfare.

One of the visible signs of this progress was the disappearance of the latrines. I hated the latrines, and I used to wonder about the sort of men who came with their lorries at night and carted away the filth; and there was always the horrible fear of falling into a pit.

One of the first men to have decent lavatories built was Hat, and we made a great thing of knocking down his old latrine. All the boys and men went to give a hand. I was too small to give a hand, but I went to watch. The walls were knocked down one by one and in the end there was only one remaining.

Hat said, "Boys, let we try to knock this one down in one big piece."

And they did.

The wall swayed and began to fall.

I must have gone mad in that split second, for I did a Superman act and tried to prevent the wall falling.

I just remember people shouting, "O God! Look out!"

I was travelling in a bus, one of the green buses of Sam's Super Service, from Port-of-Spain to Petit Valley. The bus was full of old women in bright bandanas carrying big baskets of eddoes, yams, bananas, with here and there some chickens. Suddenly the old women all began chattering, and the chickens began squawking. My head felt as though it would split, but when I tried to shout at the old women I found I couldn't open my mouth. I tried again, but all I heard, more distinctly now, was the constant chattering.

Water was pouring down my face.

I was flat out under a tap and there were faces above me looking down.

Somebody shouted, "He recover. Is all right."

Hat said, "How you feeling?"

I said, trying to laugh, "I feeling all right."

Mrs Bhakcu said, "You have any pains?"

I shook my head.

But, suddenly, my whole body began to ache. I tried to move my hand and it hurt.

I said, "I think I break my hand."

But I could stand, and they made me walk into the house.

My mother came, and I could see her eyes glassy and wet with tears.

Somebody, I cannot remember who, said, "Boy, you had your mother really worried."

I looked at her tears, and I felt I was going to cry too. I had discovered that she could be worried and anxious for me.

I wished I were a Hindu god at that moment, with two hundred arms, so that all two hundred could be broken, just to enjoy that moment, and to see again my mother's tears.

The Burglars

KENNETH GRAHAME

IT was much too fine a night to think of going to bed at once, and so, although the witching hour of 9 p.m. had struck, Edward and I were still leaning out of the open window in our nightshirts, watching the play of the cedar-branch shadows on the moonlit lawn, and planning schemes of fresh devilry for the sunshiny morrow. From below, strains of the jocund piano declared that the Olympians were enjoying themselves in their listless, impotent way; for the new curate had been bidden to dinner that night, and was at the moment unclerically proclaiming to all the world that he feared no foe. His discordant vociferations doubtless started a train of thought in Edward's mind, for he presently remarked *à propos* of nothing whatever that had been said before, "I believe the new curate's rather gone on Aunt Maria."

I scouted the notion. "Why, she's quite old," I said. (She must have seen some five-and-twenty summers.)

"Of course she is," replied Edward scornfully. "It's not her, it's her money he's after, you bet!"

"Didn't know she had any money," I observed timidly.

"Sure to have," said my brother with confidence—"heaps and heaps."

Silence ensued, both our minds being busy with the new situation thus presented: mine in wonderment at this flaw that so often declared itself in enviable natures of fullest endowment—in a grown-up man and a good cricketer, for instance, even as this curate; Edward's (apparently) in the consideration of how such a state of things, supposing it existed, could be best turned to his own advantage.

"Bobby Ferris told me," began Edward, in due course, "that there was a fellow spooning his sister once——"

"What's spooning?" I asked meekly.

"Oh, I dunno," said Edward indifferently. "It's—it's—it's just a thing they do, you know. And he used to carry notes and messages and things between 'em, and he got a shilling almost every time."

"What, from each of 'em?" I innocently inquired.

Edward looked at me with scornful pity. "Girls never have any money," he briefly explained. "But she did his exercises and got him out of rows, and told stories for him when he needed it—and much better ones than he could have made up for himself. Girls are useful in some ways. So he was living in clover, when unfortunately they went and quarrelled about something."

"Don't see what that's got to do with it," I said.

"Nor don't I," rejoined Edward. "But anyhow the notes and things stopped, and so did the shillings. Bobby was fairly cornered, for he had bought two ferrets on tick, and promised to pay a shilling a week, thinking the shillings were going on for ever, the silly young ass. So when the week was up and he was being dunned for the shilling, he went off to the fellow and said: 'Your broken-hearted Bella implores you to meet her at sundown. By the hollow oak, as of old, be it only for a moment. Do not fail!' He got all that out of some rotten book, of course. The fellow looked puzzled, and said—

"'What hollow oak? I don't know any hollow oak.'

"'Perhaps it was the Royal Oak?' said Bobby promptly, 'cos he saw he had made a slip through trusting too much to the rotten book; but this didn't seem to make the fellow any happier."

"Should think not," I said; "the Royal Oak's an awful low sort of pub."

"I know," said Edward. "Well, at last the fellow said, 'I

104

think I know what she means: the hollow tree in your father's paddock. It happens to be an elm, but she wouldn't know the difference. All right; say I'll be there.' Bobby hung about a bit, for he hadn't got his money. 'She was crying awfully,' he said. Then he got his shilling."

"And wasn't the fellow riled," I inquired, "when he got to the place and found nothing?"

"He found Bobby," said Edward indignantly. "Young Ferris was a gentleman, every inch of him. He brought the fellow another message from Bella: 'I dare not leave the house. My cruel parents immure me closely. If you only knew what I suffer!—Your broken-hearted Bella.' Out of the same rotten book. This made the fellow a little suspicious, 'cos it was the old Ferrises who had been keen about the thing all through. The fellow, you see, had tin."

"But what's that got to——" I began again.

"Oh, I dunno," said Edward impatiently. "I'm telling you just what Bobby told me. He got suspicious, anyhow, but he couldn't exactly call Bella's brother a liar, so Bobby escaped for the time. But when he was in a hole next week, over a stiff French exercise, and tried the same sort of game on his sister, she was too sharp for him, and he got caught out. Somehow women seem more mistrustful than men. They're so beastly suspicious by nature, you know."

"I know," said I. "But did the two—the fellow and the sister—make it up afterwards?"

"I don't remember about that," replied Edward indifferently; "but Bobby got packed off to school a whole year earlier than his people meant to send him. Which was just what he wanted. So you see it all came right in the end!"

I was trying to puzzle out the moral of this story—it was evidently meant to contain one somewhere—when a flood of golden lamplight mingled with the moon-rays on the lawn, and Aunt Maria and the new curate strolled out on the grass below us, and took the direction of a garden-seat which was backed by a dense laurel shrubbery reaching round in a half-circle to the house. Edward meditated moodily. "If we only knew what they were talking about," said he, "you'd soon see whether I was right or not. Look here! Let's send the kid down by the porch to reconnoitre!"

"Harold's asleep," I said; "it seems rather a shame——"

"Oh, rot!" said my brother; "he's the youngest, and he's got to do as he's told!"

So the luckless Harold was hauled out of bed and given his sailing orders. He was naturally rather vexed at being stood up suddenly on the cold floor, and the job had no particular interest for him; but he was both staunch and well-disciplined. The means of exit were simple enough. A porch of iron trellis came up to within easy reach of the window, and was habitually used by all three of us when modestly anxious to avoid public notice. Harold climbed deftly down the porch like a white rat, and his nightgown glimmered a moment on the gravel walk ere he was lost to sight in the darkness of the shrubbery. A brief interval of silence ensued, broken suddenly by a sound of scuffle, and then a shrill, long-drawn squeal, as of metallic surfaces in friction. Our scout had fallen into the hands of the enemy.

Indolence alone had made us devolve the task of investigation on our younger brother. Now that danger had declared itself, there was no hesitation. In a second we were down the side of the porch, and crawling Cherokee-wise through the laurels to the back of the garden-seat. Piteous was the sight that greeted us. Aunt Maria was on the seat, in a white evening frock, looking—for an aunt—really quite nice. On the lawn stood an incensed curate, grasping our small brother by a large ear, which—judging from the row he was making—seemed on the point of parting company with the head it completed and adorned. The gruesome noise he was emitting did not really affect us otherwise than aesthetically. To one who has tried both, the wail of genuine physical anguish is easily distinguishable from the pumped-up *ad misericordiam* blubber. Harold's could clearly be recognized as belonging to the latter class. "Now you young—" (whelp, I think it was, but Edward stoutly maintains it was devil), said the curate sternly, "tell us what you mean by it!"

"Well, leggo of my ear then," shrilled Harold, "and I'll tell you the solemn truth!"

"Very well," agreed the curate, releasing him; "now go ahead, and don't lie more than you can help."

We abode the promised disclosure without the least misgiving; but even we had hardly given Harold due credit for his fertility of resource and powers of imagination.

"I had just finished saying my prayers," began that young gentleman slowly, "when I happened to look out of the window, and on the lawn I saw a sight which froze the marrow in my veins! A burglar was approaching the house with snake-like tread! He had a scowl and a dark lantern, and he was armed to the teeth!"

We listened with interest. The style, though unlike Harold's native notes, seemed strangely familiar.

"Go on," said the curate grimly.

"Pausing in his stealthy career," continued Harold, "he gave a low whistle. Instantly the signal was responded to, and from the adjacent shadows two more figures glided forth. The miscreants were both armed to the teeth."

"Excellent," said the curate: "proceed."

"The robber chief," pursued Harold, warming to his work, "joined his nefarious comrades, and conversed with them in silent tones. His expression was truly ferocious, and I ought to have said that he was armed to the t——"

"There, never mind his teeth," interrupted the curate rudely; "there's too much jaw about you altogether. Hurry up and have done."

"I was in a frightful funk," continued the narrator, warily guarding his ear with his hand; "but just then the drawing-room window opened, and you and Aunt Maria came out—I mean emerged. The burglars vanished silently into the laurels, with horrid implications!"

The curate looked slightly puzzled. The tale was well sustained, and certainly circumstantial. After all, the boy might really have seen something. How was the poor man to know—though the chaste and lofty diction might have supplied a hint—that the whole yarn was a free adaptation from the last Penny Dreadful lent us by the knife-and-boot boy?

"Why did you not alarm the house?" he asked.

"'Cos I was afraid," said Harold sweetly, "that p'raps they mightn't believe me."

"But how did you get down here, you naughty little boy?" put in Aunt Maria.

Harold was hard pressed—by his own flesh and blood, too!

At that moment Edward touched me on the shoulder and glided off through the laurels. When some ten yards away he gave a low whistle. I replied with another. The effect was magical. Aunt Maria started up with a shriek. Harold gave one startled glance around, and then fled like a hare, made straight for the back door, burst in upon the servants at supper, and buried himself in the broad bosom of the cook, his special ally. The curate faced the laurels—hesitatingly. But Aunt Maria flung herself on him. "O Mr Hodgitts," I heard her cry, "you are brave! for my sake do not be rash!" He was not rash. When I peeped out a second later the coast was entirely clear.

By this time there were sounds of a household timidly emerging, and Edward remarked to me that perhaps we had better be off. Retreat was an easy matter. A stunted laurel gave a leg-up on to the garden wall, which led in its turn to the roof of an outhouse, up which, at a dubious angle, we could crawl to the window of the box-room. This overland route had been revealed to us one day by the domestic cat, when hard pressed in the course of an otter-hunt, in which the cat—somewhat unwillingly—was filling the title rôle; and it had proved distinctly useful on occasions like the present. We were snug in bed—minus some cuticle from knees and elbows—and Harold, sleepily chewing something

sticky, had been carried up in the arms of the friendly cook
ere the clamour of the burglar-hunters had died away.

The curate's undaunted demeanour, as reported by Aunt
Maria, was generally supposed to have terrified the burglars
into flight, and much kudos accrued to him thereby. Some
days later, however, when he had dropped in to afternoon tea,
and was making a mild curatorial joke about the moral
courage required for taking the last piece of bread-and-butter,
I felt constrained to remark dreamily, and as it were to the
universe at large, "Mr Hodgitts, you are brave! for my sake
do not be rash!"

Fortunately for me, the vicar also was a caller on that day;
and it was always a comparatively easy matter to dodge my
long-coated friend in the open.

Holding Her Down

JACK LONDON

BARRING accidents, a good hobo, with youth and agility, can hold a train down despite all the efforts of the train-crew to "ditch" him—given, of course, night-time as an essential condition. When such a hobo, under such conditions, makes up his mind that he is going to hold her down, either he does hold her down, or chance trips him up. There is no legitimate way, short of murder, whereby the train-crew can ditch him. That train-crews have not stopped short of murder is a current belief in the tramp world. Not having had that particular experience in my tramp days I cannot vouch for it personally.

But this I have heard of the "bad" roads. When a tramp has "gone underneath", on the rods, and the train is in motion, there is apparently no way of dislodging him until the train stops. The tramp, snugly ensconced inside the truck, with the four wheels and all the frame-work around him, has the "cinch" on the crew—or so he thinks, until some day he rides the rods on a bad road. A bad road is usually one on which a short time previously one or several trainmen have been killed by tramps. Heaven pity the tramp who is caught "underneath" on such a road—for caught he is, though the train be going sixty miles an hour.

The "shack" (brakeman) takes a coupling-pin and a length of bell-cord to the platform in front of the truck in which the tramp is riding. The shack fastens the coupling pin to the bell-cord, drops the former down between the platforms, and pays out the latter. The coupling-pin strikes the ties between the rails, rebounds against the bottom of the car, and again strikes the ties. The shack plays it back and forth, now to this side, now to the other, lets it out a bit and hauls it in a bit, giving his weapon opportunity for every variety of impact and rebound. Every blow of that flying coupling-pin is freighted with death, and at sixty miles an hour it beats a veritable tattoo of death. The next day the remains of that tramp are gathered up along the right of way, and a line in the local paper mentions the unknown man, undoubtedly a tramp, assumably drunk, who had probably fallen asleep on the track.

As a characteristic illustration of how a capable hobo can hold her down, I am minded to give the following experience. I was in Ottawa, bound west over the Canadian Pacific. Three thousand miles of that road stretched before me; it was the fall of the year, and I had to cross Manitoba and the Rocky Mountains. I could expect "crimpy" weather, and every moment of delay increased the frigid hardships of the journey. Furthermore, I was disgusted. The distance between Montreal and Ottawa is one hundred and twenty miles. I ought to know, for I had just come over it, and it had taken me six days. By mistake I had missed the main line and come over a small "jerk" with only two locals a day on it. And during these six days I had lived on dry crusts, and not enough of them, begged from the French peasants.

Furthermore, my disgust had been heightened by the one day I had spent in Ottawa trying to get an outfit of clothing for my long journey. Let me put it on record right here that Ottawa, with one exception, is the hardest town in the United States and Canada to beg clothes in; the one exception is Washington D.C. The latter fair city is the limit. I spent two weeks there trying to beg a pair of shoes, and then had to go on to Jersey City before I got them.

But to return to Ottawa. At eight sharp in the morning I started out after clothes. I worked energetically all day. I swear I walked forty miles. I interviewed the housewives of a thousand homes. I did not even knock off work for dinner.

And at six in the afternoon, after ten hours of unremitting and depressing toil, I was still shy one shirt, while the pair of trousers I had managed to acquire was tight and, moreover, was showing all the signs of an early disintegration.

At six I quit work and headed for the railroad yards, expecting to pick up something to eat on the way. But my hard luck was still with me. I was refused food at house after house. Then I got a "hand-out". My spirits soared, for it was the largest hand-out I had ever seen in a long and varied experience. It was a parcel wrapped in newspapers and as big as a mature suit-case. I hurried to a vacant lot and opened it. First, I saw cake, then more cake, all kinds and makes of cake, and then some. It was all cake. No bread and butter with thick firm slices of meat between—nothing but cake; and I who of all things abhorred cake most! In another age and clime they sat down by the waters of Babylon and wept. And in a vacant lot in Canada's proud capital, I, too, sat down and wept . . . over a mountain of cake. As one looks upon the face of his dead son, so looked I upon that multitudinous pastry. I suppose I was an ungrateful tramp, for I refused to partake of the bounteousness of the house that had had a party the night before. Evidently the guests hadn't liked cake either.

That cake marked the crisis in my fortunes. Than it nothing could be worse; therefore things must begin to mend. And they did. At the very next house I was given a "set-down". Now a "set-down" is the height of bliss. One is taken inside, very often is given a chance to wash, and is then "set-down" at a table. Tramps love to throw their legs under a table. The house was large and comfortable, in the midst of spacious grounds and fine trees, and sat well back from the street. They had just finished eating, and I was taken right into the dining-room—in itself a most unusual happening, for the tramp who is lucky enough to win a "set-down" usually receives it in the kitchen. A grizzled and gracious Englishman, his matronly wife, and a beautiful young Frenchwoman talked with me while I ate.

I wonder if that beautiful young Frenchwoman would remember, at this late day, the laugh I gave her when I uttered the barbaric phrase, "two bits". You see, I was trying delicately to hit them for a "light piece". That was how the sum of money came to be mentioned. "What?" she said. "Two bits", said I. Her mouth was twitching as she again said, "What?" "Two bits", said I. Whereat she burst into laughter. "Won't you repeat it?" she said, when she had regained control of herself. "Two bits", said I. And once more she rippled into uncontrollable silvery laughter. "I beg your pardon," said she, "but what . . . what was it you said?" "Two bits", said I. "Is there anything wrong about it?" "Not that I know of," she gurgled between gasps, "but what does it mean?" I explained, but I do not remember now whether or not I got that two bits out of her; but I have often wondered since as to which of us was the provincial.

When I arrived at the depot, I found much to my disgust, a bunch of at least twenty tramps that were waiting to ride out the blind baggages of the overland. Now two or three tramps on the blind baggages are all right. They are inconspicuous. But a score! That meant trouble. No train-crew would ever let all of us ride.

I may as well explain here what a blind baggage is. Some mail-cars are built without doors in the ends; hence, such a car is "blind". The mail-cars that possess end doors, have those doors always locked. Suppose, after the train has started, that a tramp gets on to the platform of one of these blind cars. There is no door, or the door is locked. No conductor or brakeman can get to him to collect fare or throw him off. It is clear that the tramp is safe until the next time the train stops. Then he must get off, run ahead in the darkness, and when the train pulls by, jump on to the blind again. But there are ways and ways, as you shall see.

When the train pulled out, those twenty tramps swarmed upon the three blinds. Some climbed on before the train had run a car-length. They were awkward dubs, and I saw their speedy finish. Of course, the train-crew was "on", and at the first stop the trouble began. I jumped off and ran forward along the track. I noticed that I was accompanied by a number of the tramps. They evidently knew their business. When one is beating an overland, he must always keep well ahead of the train at the stops. I ran ahead, and as I ran, one by one those that accompanied me dropped out. This dropping out was the measure of their skill and nerve in boarding a train.

For this is the way it works. When the train starts, the shack rides out the blind. There is no way for him to get back into the train proper except by jumping off the blind and catching a platform where the car-ends are not "blind". When the train is going as fast as the shack cares to risk, he therefore jumps off the blind, lets several cars go by, and gets on to the train. So it is up to the tramp to run so far ahead that before the blind is opposite him the shack will have already vacated it.

I dropped the last tramp by about fifty feet, and waited. The train started. I saw the lantern of the shack on the first blind. He was riding her out. And I saw the dubs stand forlornly by the track as the blind went by. They made no attempt to get on. They were beaten by their own inefficiency at the very start. After them, in the line-up, came the tramps that knew a little something about the game. They let the first blind, occupied by the shack, go by, and jumped on the second and third blinds. Of course, the shack jumped off the first and on the second as it went by, and scrambled around there, throwing off the men who had boarded it. But the point is that I was so far ahead that when the first blind came opposite me, the shack had already left it and was tangled up with the tramps on the second blind. A half dozen of the more skilful tramps, who had run far enough ahead, made the first blind, too.

At the next stop, as we ran forward along the track, I counted but fifteen of us. Five had been ditched. The weeding-out process had begun nobly, and it continued station by

114

station. Now we were fourteen, now twelve, now eleven, now nine, now eight. It reminded me of the ten little niggers of the nursery rhyme. I was resolved that I should be the last little nigger of all. And why not? Was I not blessed with strength, agility, and youth? (I was eighteen and in perfect condition.) And didn't I have my "nerve" with me? And furthermore, was I not a tramp-royal? Were not these other tramps mere dubs and "gay-cats" and amateurs alongside of me? If I weren't the last little nigger, I might as well quit the game and get a job on an alfalfa farm somewhere.

By the time our number had been reduced to four, the whole train-crew had become interested. From then on it was a contest of skill and wits, with the odds in favour of the crew. One by one the three other survivors turned up missing, until I alone remained. My, but I was proud of myself! No Crœsus was ever prouder of his first million. I was holding her down in spite of two brakemen, a conductor, a fireman, and an engineer.

And here are a few samples of the way I held her down. Out ahead, in the darkness—so far ahead that the shack riding out the blind must perforce get off before it reaches me—I get on. Very well. I am good for another station. When that station is reached, I dart ahead again to repeat the manœuvre. The train pulls out. I watch her coming. There is no light of a lantern on the blind. Has the crew abandoned the fight? I do not know. One never knows, and one must be prepared every moment for anything. As the first blind comes opposite me, and I run to leap aboard, I strain my eyes to see if the shack is on the platform. For all I know he may be there, with his lantern doused, and even as I spring upon the steps that lantern may even smash down upon my head. I ought to know. I have been hit by lanterns two or three times.

But no, the first blind is empty. The train is gathering speed. I am safe for another station. But am I? I feel the train slacken speed. On the instant I am alert. A manœuvre is being executed against me, and I do not know what it is. I try to

115

watch on both sides at once, not forgetting to keep track of the tender in front of me. From any one, or all, of these three directions, I may be assailed.

Ah, there it comes. The shack has ridden out the engine. My first warning is when his feet strike the steps of the right-hand side of the blind. Like a flash I am off the blind to the left and running ahead past the engine. I lose myself in the darkness. The situation is where it has been ever since the train left Ottawa. I am ahead, and the train must come past me if it is to proceed on its journey. I have as good a chance as ever for boarding her.

I watch carefully. I see a lantern come forward to the engine, and I do not see it go back from the engine. It must therefore be still on the engine, and it is a fair assumption that attached to the handle of that lantern is a shack. That shack was lazy, or else he would have put out his lantern instead of trying to shield it as he came forward. The train pulls out. The first blind is empty, and I gain it. As before, the train slackens, the shack from the engine boards the blind from one side, and I go off the other side and run forward.

As I wait in the darkness I am conscious of a big thrill of pride. The overland has stopped twice for me—for me, a poor hobo on the bum. I alone have twice stopped the overland with its many passengers and coaches, its government mail, and its two thousand steam horses straining in the engine. And I weigh only one hundred and sixty pounds, and I haven't a five-cent piece in my pocket!

Again I see the lantern come forward to the engine. But this time it comes conspicuously. A bit too conspicuously to suit me, and I wonder what is up. At any rate I have something else to be afraid of than the shack on the engine. The train pulls by. Just in time, before I make my spring, I see the dark form of a shack, without a lantern, on the first blind. I let it go by, and prepare to board the second blind. But the shack on the first blind has jumped off and is at my heels. Also, I have a fleeting glimpse of the lantern of the shack who rode out the engine. He has jumped off, and now both shacks are on the ground on the same side with me. The next moment the second blind comes by and I am aboard it. But I do not linger. I have figured out my countermove. As I dash across the platform I hear the impact of the shack's feet against the steps as he boards. I jump off the other side and run forward with the train. My plan is to run forward and get on the first blind. It is nip and tuck, for the train is gathering speed. Also, the shack is behind me and running after me. I guess I am the better sprinter, for I make the first blind. I stand on the steps and watch my pursuer. He is only about ten feet back and running hard; but now the train has approximated his own speed, and, relative to me, he is standing still. I encourage him, hold out my hand to him; but he explodes in a mighty oath, gives up and makes the train several cars back.

The train is speeding along, and I am still chuckling to myself, when, without warning, a spray of water strikes me. The fireman is playing the hose on me from the engine. I step forward from the car-platform to the rear of the tender, where I am sheltered under the overhang. The water flies harmlessly over my head. My fingers itch to climb up on the tender and lam that fireman with a chunk of coal; but I know if I do that, I'll be massacred by him and the engineer, and I refrain.

At the next stop I am off and ahead in the darkness. This time, when the train pulls out, both shacks are on the first blind. I divine their game. They have blocked the repetition of my previous play. I cannot again take the second blind, cross over, and run forward to the first. As soon as the first blind passes and I do not get on, they swing off, one on each side of the train. I board the second blind, and as I do so I know that a moment later, simultaneously, those two shacks will arrive on both sides of me. It is like a trap. Both ways are blocked. Yet there is another way out, and that way is up.

So I do not wait for my pursuers to arrive. I climb upon the upright ironwork of the platform and stand upon the wheel of the sand-brake. This has taken up the moment of grace and

I hear the shacks strike the steps on either side. I don't stop to look. I raise my arms overhead until my hands rest against the down-curving ends of the roofs of the two cars. One hand, of course, is on the curved roof of one car, the other hand on the curved roof of the other car. By this time both shacks are coming up the steps. I know it, though I am too busy to see them... All this is happening in the space of only several seconds. I make a spring with my legs, and "muscle" myself up with my arms. As I draw up my legs, both shacks reach for me and clutch empty air. I know this, for I look down and see them. Also I hear them swear.

I am now in a precarious position, riding the ends of the down-curving roofs of two cars at the same time. With a quick, tense movement, I transfer both legs to the curve of one roof and both hands to the curve of the other roof. Then, gripping the edge of that curving roof, I climb over the curve to the level roof above, where I sit down to catch my breath, holding on the while to a ventilator that projects above the surface. I am on top of the train—on the "decks", as the tramps call it, and this process I have described is by them called "decking her". And let me say right here that only a young and vigorous tramp is able to deck a passenger train, and also, that the young and vigorous tramp must have his nerve with him as well.

The train goes on gathering speed, and I know I am safe until the next stop—but only until the next stop. If I remain on the roof after the train stops, I know those shacks will fusillade me with rocks. A healthy shack can "dewdrop" a pretty heavy chunk of stone on top of a car—say anywhere from five to twenty pounds. On the other hand, the chances are large that at the next stop the shacks will be waiting for me to descend at the place I climbed up. It is up to me to climb down at some other platform.

Registering a fervent hope that there are no tunnels in the next half mile, I rise to my feet and walk down the train half a dozen cars. And let me say that one must leave timidity behind him on such a *passear*. The roofs of passenger coaches are not made for midnight promenades. And if any one thinks they are, let me advise him to try it. Just let him walk along the roof of a jolting, lurching car, with nothing to hold on to but the black and empty air, and when he comes to the down-curving end of the roof, all wet and slippery with dew, let him accelerate his speed so as to step across to the next roof, down-curving and wet and slippery. Believe me, he will learn whether his heart is weak, or his head is giddy.

As the train slows down for a stop, half a dozen platforms from where I had decked her I come down. No one is on the platform. When the train comes to a standstill, I slip off to the ground. Ahead, and between me and the engine, are two moving lanterns. The shacks are looking for me on the roofs of the cars. I note that the car beside which I am standing is a "four-wheeler"—by which is meant that it has only four wheels to each truck. (When you go underneath on the rods, be sure to avoid the "six-wheelers"—they lead to disasters.)

I duck under the train and make for the rods, and I can tell you I am mighty glad that the train is standing still. It is the first time I have ever gone underneath on the Canadian Pacific, and the internal arrangements are new to me. I try to crawl over the top of the truck, between the truck and the bottom of the car. But the space is not large enough for me to squeeze through. This is new to me. Down in the United States I am accustomed to going underneath on rapidly-moving trains, seizing a gunnel and swinging my feet under the brake-beam, and from there crawling over the top of the truck and down inside the truck to a seat on the cross-rod.

Feeling with my hands in the darkness, I learn that there is room between the brake-beam and the ground. It is a tight squeeze. I have to lie flat and worm my way through. Once inside the truck, I take my seat on the rod and wonder what the shacks are thinking has become of me. The train gets under way. They have given me up at last.

But have they? At the very next stop, I see a lantern thrust under the next truck to mine at the other end of the car. They are searching the rods for me. I must make my get-away pretty lively. I crawl on my stomach under the brake-beam. They see me and run for me, but I crawl on hands and knees across the rail on the opposite side and gain my feet. Then away I go for the head of the train. I run past the engine and hide in the sheltering darkness. It is the same old situation. I am ahead of the train, and the train must go past me.

The train pulls out. There is a lantern on the first blind. I lie low, and see the peering shack go by. But there is also a lantern on the second blind. That shack spots me and calls to the shack who has gone past on the first blind. Both jump off. Never mind, I'll take the third blind and deck her. But heavens, there is a lantern on the third blind, too. It is the conductor. I let it go by. At any rate I have now the full train-crew in front of me. I turn and run back in the opposite direction to what the train is going. I look over my shoulder. All three lanterns are on the ground and wobbling along in pursuit. I sprint. Half the train has gone by, and it is going quite fast, when I spring aboard. I know that the two shacks and the conductor will arrive like ravening wolves in about two seconds. I spring upon the wheel of the hand-brake, get my hands on the curved ends of the roofs, and muscle myself up to the decks; while my disappointed pursuers, clustering on the platform beneath like dogs that have treed a cat, howl curses up at me and say unsocial things about my ancestors.

But what does that matter? It is five to one, including the engineer and fireman, and the majesty of the law and the might of a great corporation are behind them, and I am beating them out. I am too far down the train, and I run ahead over the roofs of the coaches until I am over the fifth or sixth platform from the engine. I peer down cautiously. A shack is on the platform. That he has caught sight of me, I know from the way he makes a swift sneak inside the car; and I know, also, that he is waiting inside the door, all ready to pounce on me when I climb down. But I make believe that I don't know, and I remain there to encourage him in his error. I do not see him, yet I know that he opens the door once and peeps up to assure himself that I am still there.

The train slows down for a station. I dangle my legs down in a tentative way. The train stops. My legs are still dangling. I hear the door unlatch softly. He is all ready for me. Suddenly I spring up and run forward over the roof. This is right over his head, where he lurks inside the door. The train is standing still; the night is quiet, and I take care to make plenty of noise on the metal roof with my feet. I don't know, but my assumption is that he is now running forward to catch me as I descend at the next platform. But I don't descend there. Halfway along the roof of the coach, I turn, retrace my way softly and quickly to the platform both the shack and I have just abandoned. The coast is clear. I descend to the ground on the off-side of the train and hide in the darkness. Not a soul has seen me.

I go over to the fence, at the edge of the right of way, and watch. Ah, ha! What's that? I see a lantern on top of the train, moving along from front to rear. They think I haven't come down, and they are searching the roofs for me. And better than that—on the ground on each side of the train, moving abreast with the lantern on top, are two other lanterns. It is a rabbit-drive, and I am the rabbit. When the shack on top flushes me, the ones on each side will nab me. I roll a cigarette and watch the procession go by. Once past me, I am safe to proceed to the front of the train. She pulls out, and I make the front blind without opposition. But before she is fully under way and just as I am lighting my cigarette, I am aware that the fireman has climbed over the coal to the back of the tender and is looking down on me. I am filled with apprehension. From his position he can mash me to a jelly with lumps of coal. Instead of which he addresses me, and I note with relief the admiration in his voice.

"You son-of-a-gun," is what he says.

It is a high compliment, and I thrill as a schoolboy thrills on receiving a reward of merit.

"Say," I call up to him, "don't you play the hose on me any more."

"All right," he answers, and goes back to his work.

I have made friends with the engine, but the shacks are still looking for me. At the next stop, the shacks ride out all three blinds, and as before, I let them go by and deck in the middle of the train. The crew is on its mettle by now, and the train stops. The shacks are going to ditch me or know the reason why. Three times the mighty overland stops for me at that station, and each time I elude the shacks and make the decks. But it is hopeless, for they have finally come to an understanding of the situation. I have taught them that they cannot guard the train from me. They must do something else.

And they do it. When the train stops that last time, they take after me hot-footed. Ah, I see their game. They are trying to run me down. At first they herd me back towards the rear of the train. I know my peril. Once to the rear of the train, it will pull out with me left behind. I double, and twist, and turn, dodge through my pursuers, and gain the front of the train. One shack still hangs on after me. All right, I'll give him the run of his life, for my wind is good. I run straight ahead along the track. It doesn't matter. If he chases me ten miles, he'll nevertheless have to catch the train, and I can board her at any speed that he can.

So I run on, keeping just comfortably ahead of him and straining my eyes in the gloom for cattle-guards and switches that may bring me to grief. Alas! I strain my eyes too far ahead, and trip over something just under my feet, I know not what, some little thing, and go down to earth in a long, stumbling fall. The next moment I am on my feet, but the shack has me by the collar. I do not struggle. I am busy with breathing deeply and with sizing him up. He is narrow-shouldered, and I have at least thirty pounds the better of him in weight. Besides, he is just as tired as I am, and if he tries to slug me, I'll teach him a few things.

But he doesn't try to slug me, and that problem is settled. Instead, he starts to lead me back towards the train, and another possible problem arises. I see the lanterns of the conductor and the other shack. We are approaching them. Not for nothing have I made the acquaintance of the New York police. Not for nothing, in box-cars, by water-tanks, and in prison-cells, have I listened to bloody tales of man-handling. What if these three men are about to man-handle me? Heaven knows I have given them provocation enough. I think quickly. We are drawing nearer and nearer to the other two trainmen. I line up the stomach and the jaw of my captor and plan the right and left I'll give him at the first sign of trouble.

Pshaw! I know another trick I'd like to work on him, and almost regret that I did not do it at the moment I was captured. I could make him sick, what of his clutch on my collar. My coat is tightly buttoned. Did you ever see a tourniquet? Well, this is one. All I have to do is to duck my head under his arm and begin to twist. I must twist rapidly—very rapidly. I know how to do it; twisting in a violent, jerky way, ducking my head under his arm with each revolution. Before he knows it, those detaining fingers of his will be detained. He will be unable to withdraw them. It is a powerful leverage. Twenty seconds after I have started revolving, the blood will be bursting out of his finger ends, the delicate tendons will be rupturing, and all the muscles and nerves will be mashing and crushing together in a shrieking mass. Try it sometimes when somebody has you by the collar. But be quick—quick as lightning. Also, be sure to hug yourself while you are revolving—hug your face with your left arm and your abdomen with your right. You see, the other fellow might try to stop you with a punch from his free arm. It would be a good idea, too, to revolve away from that free arm rather than towards it. A punch going is never so bad as a punch coming.

That shack will never know how near he was to being made

123

very, very sick. All that saves him is that it is not in their plan to man-handle me. When we draw near enough, he calls out that he has me, and they signal the train to come on. The engine passes us, and the three blinds. After that, the conductor and the other shack swing aboard. But still my captor holds on to me. I see the plan. He is going to hold me until the rear of the train goes by. Then he will hop on, and I shall be left behind—ditched.

But the train has pulled out fast, the engineer trying to make up for lost time. Also, it is a long train. It is going very lively, and I know the shack is measuring its speed with apprehension.

"Think you can make it?" I query innocently.

He releases my collar, makes a quick run, and swings aboard. A number of coaches are yet to pass by. He knows it, and remains on the steps, his head poked out and watching me. In that moment my next move comes to me. I'll make the last platform. I know she's going fast and faster, but I'll only get a roll in the dirt if I fail, and the optimism of youth is mine. I do not give myself away. I stand with a dejected droop of shoulder, advertising that I have abandoned hope. But at the same time I am feeling with my feet the good gravel. It is perfect footing. Also I am watching the poked-out head of the shack. I see it withdrawn. He is confident that the train is going too fast for me ever to make it.

And the train *is* going fast—faster than any train I have ever tackled. As the last coach comes by I sprint in the same direction with it. It is a swift, short sprint. I cannot hope to equal the speed of the train, but I can reduce the difference of our speed to the minimum, and, hence, reduce the shock of impact, when I leap on board. In the fleeting instant of darkness I do not see the iron hand-rail of the last platform; nor is there time for me to locate it. I reach for where I think it ought to be, and at the same instant my feet leave the ground. It is all in the toss. The next moment I may be rolling in the gravel with broken ribs, or arms, or head. But my fingers grip the handhold, there is a jerk on my arms that slightly pivots my body, and my feet land on the steps with sharp violence.

I sit down, feeling very proud of myself. In all my hoboing it is the best bit of train-jumping I have done. I know that late at night one is always good for several stations on the last platform, but I do not care to trust myself at the rear of the train. At the first stop I run forward on the off-side of the train, pass the Pullmans, and duck under and take a rod under a day-coach. At the next stop I run forward again and take another rod.

I am now comparatively safe. The shacks think I am ditched. But the long day and the strenuous night are beginning to tell on me. Also, it is not so windy nor cold underneath, and I begin to doze. This will never do. Sleep on the rods spells death, so I crawl out at a station and forward to the second blind. Here I can lie down and sleep; and here I do sleep—how long I do not know—for I am awakened by a lantern thrust into my face. The two shacks are staring at me. I scramble up on the defensive, wondering as to which one is going to make the first "pass" at me. But slugging is far from their minds.

"I thought you was ditched," says the shack who had held me by the collar.

"If you hadn't let go of me when you did, you'd have been ditched along with me," I answer.

"How's that?" he asks.

"I'd have gone into a clinch with you, that's all," is my reply.

They hold a consultation, and their verdict is summed-up in, "Well, I guess you can ride, Bo. There's no use trying to keep you off."

And they go away and leave me in peace to the end of their division.

I have given the foregoing as a sample of what "holding her down" means. Of course, I have selected a fortunate night out of my experiences, and said nothing of the nights—and many of them—when I was tripped up by accident and ditched.

In conclusion, I want to tell of what happened when I reached the end of the division. On single-track, transcontinental lines, the freight trains wait at the divisions and follow out after the passenger trains. When the divisions was reached, I left my train, and looked for the freight that would pull out behind it. I found the freight made up on a side-track and waiting. I climbed into a box-car half full of coal and lay down. In no time I was asleep.

I was awakened by the sliding open of the door. Day was just dawning, cold and grey, and the freight had not yet started. A "con" (conductor) was poking his head inside the door.

"Get out of that, you blankety-blank-blank!" he roared at me.

I got, and outside I watched him go down the line inspecting every car in the train. When he got out of sight I thought to myself that he would never think I'd have the nerve to climb back into the very car out of which he had fired me. So back I climbed and lay down again.

Now that con's mental processes must have been paralleling mine, for he reasoned that it was the very thing I would do. For back he came and fired me out.

Now, surely, I reasoned, he will never dream that I'd do it a third time. Back I went, into the very same car. But I decided to make sure. Only one sidedoor could be opened. The other side-door was nailed up. Beginning at the top of the coal, I dug a hole alongside of that door and lay down in it. I heard the other door open. The con climbed up and looked in over the top of the coal. He couldn't see me. He called to me to get out. I tried to fool him by remaining quiet. But when he began tossing chunks of coal into the hole on top of me, I gave up and for the third time was fired out. Also, he informed me in warm terms of what would happen to me if he caught me in there again.

I changed my tactics. When a man is paralleling your mental processes, ditch him. Abruptly break off your line of reasoning and go off on a new line. This I did. I hid between some cars on an adjacent side-track, and watched. Sure enough, that con came back again to the car. He opened the door, he climbed up, he called, he threw coal into the hole I had made. He even crawled over the coal and looked into the hole. That satisfied him. Five minutes later the freight was pulling out, and he was not in sight. I ran alongside the car, pulled the door open and climbed in. He never looked for me again, and I rode that coal-car precisely one thousand and twenty-two miles, sleeping most of the time and getting out at divisions (where the freights always stop for an hour or so) to beg my food. And at the end of the thousand and twenty-two miles I lost that car through a happy incident. I got a "set-down", and the tramp doesn't live who won't miss a train for a set-down any time.

The Vertical Ladder

WILLIAM SANSOM

AS he felt the first watery eggs of sweat moistening the palms of his hands, as with every rung higher his body seemed to weigh more heavily, this young man Flegg regretted in sudden desperation, but still in vain, the irresponsible events that had thrust him up into his present precarious climb. Here he was, isolated on a vertical iron ladder flat to the side of a gasometer and bound to climb higher and higher until he should reach the vertiginous skyward summit.

How could he ever have wished this on himself? How easy it had been to laugh away his cautionary fears on the firm ground . . . now he would give the very hands that clung to the ladder for a safe conduct to solid earth.

It had been a strong spring day, abruptly as warm as midsummer. The sun flooded the parks and streets with sudden heat—Flegg and his friends had felt stifled in their thick winter clothes. The green glare of the new leaves everywhere struck the eye too fiercely, the air seemed almost sticky from the exhalations of buds and swelling resins. Cold winter senses were overcome—the girls had complained of headaches—and their thoughts had grown confused and uncomfortable as the wool underneath against their skins. They had wandered out from the park by a back gate, into an area of back streets.

The houses there were small and old, some of them already falling into disrepair; short streets, cobbles, narrow pavements, and the only shops a tobacconist or a desolate corner oil-shop to colour the grey—it was the outcrop of some industrial undertaking beyond. At first these quiet, almost deserted streets had seemed more restful than the park; but soon a dusty air of peeling plaster and powdering brick, the dark windows and the dry stone steps, the very dryness altogether had proved more wearying than before, so that when suddenly the houses ended and the ground opened to reveal the yards of a disused gasworks, Flegg and his friends had welcomed the green of nettles and milkwort that grew among the scrap-iron and broken brick.

They walked out into the wasteland, the two girls and Flegg and the other two boys, and stood presently before the old gasometer itself. Among the ruined sheds this was the only erection still whole, it still predominated over the yards, towering high above other buildings for hundreds of feet around. So they threw bricks against its rusted sides.

The rust flew off in flakes and the iron rang dully. Flegg, who wished to excel in the eyes of the dark-haired girl, began throwing his bricks higher than the others, at the same time lobbing them, to suggest that he knew something of grenade-throwing, claiming for himself vicariously the glamour of a uniform. He felt the girl's eyes follow his shoulders, his shoulders broadened. She had black eyes, unshadowed beneath short wide-awake lids, as bright as a boy's eyes; her lips pouted with difficulty over a scramble of irregular teeth, so that it often looked as if she were laughing; she always frowned— and Flegg liked her earnest, purposeful expression. Altogether she seemed a wide-awake girl who would be the first to appreciate an active sort of a man. Now she frowned and shouted, "Bet you can't climb as high as you can throw!"

Then there began one of those uneasy jokes, innocent at first, that taken seriously can accumulate an hysterical accumulation of spite. Everyone recognizes this underlying unpleasantness, it is plainly felt; but just because of this the joke must at all costs be pressed forward, one becomes frightened, one laughs all the louder, pressing to drown the embarrassments of danger and guilt. The third boy had instantly shouted, "Course he can't, he can't climb no higher than himself."

Flegg turned round scoffing, so that the girl had quickly shouted again, laughing shrilly and pointing upwards. Already all five of them felt uneasy. Then in quick succession, all in a few seconds, the third boy had repeated, "Course he bloody can't." Flegg had said, "Climb to the top of anything." The other boy had said, "Climb to the top of my aunt Fanny." The girl had said, "Climb to the top of the gasworks then."

Flegg had said, "That's nothing." And the girl, pressing on then as she had to, suddenly introduced the inevitable detail that made these suppositions into fact, "Go on then, climb it. Here—tie my hanky on the top. Tie my flag to the top."

Even then Flegg had a second's chance. It occurred to him instantly that he could laugh it off; but an hysterical emphasis now possessed the girl's face—she was dancing up and down and clapping her hands insistently—and this confused Flegg. He began stuttering after the right words. But the words refused to come. At all costs he had to cover his stuttering. So, "Off we go then!" he had said. And he had turned to the gasometer.

It was not, after all, so very high. It was hardly a full-size gasometer, its trellised iron top-rail would have stood level with the roof-coping of a five or six storey tenement. Until then Flegg had only seen the gasometer as a rough mass of iron, but now every detail sprang into abrupt definition. He studied it intently, alertly considering its size and every feature of stability, the brown rusted iron sheeting smeared here and there with red lead, a curious buckling that sometimes deflated its curved bulk as though a vacuum were collapsing it from within, and the ladders scaling the sides flush with the sheeting. The grid of girders, a complexity of struts, the bolting.

There were two ladders, one Jacob's ladder clamped fast to the side, another that was more of a staircase, zigzagging up the belly of the gasometer in easy gradients and provided with a safety rail. This must have been erected later as a substitute for the Jacob's ladder, which demanded an unnecessarily stringent climb and was now in fact in disuse, for some twenty feet of its lower rungs had been torn away; however, there was apparently some painting in progress, for a wooden painter's ladder had been propped beneath with its head reaching to the undamaged bottom of the vertical ladder— the ascent was thus serviceable again. Flegg looked quickly at the foot of the wooden ladder—was it well grounded?—and then at the head farther up—was this secure?—and then up to the top, screwing his eyes to note any fault in the iron rungs reaching innumerably and indistinctly, like the dizzying strata of a zip, to the summit platform.

Flegg, rapidly assessing these structures, never stopped sauntering forward. He was committed, and so while deliberately sauntering to appear thus the more at ease, he knew that he must never hesitate. The two boys and his own girl kept up a chorus of encouraging abuse. "How I climbed Mount Everest," they shouted. "He'll come down quicker'n he went up." "Mind you don't bang your head on a harp, Sir Galahad." But the second girl had remained quiet throughout; she was already frightened, sensing instantly that the guilt for some tragedy was hers alone—although she had never in fact opened her mouth. Now she chewed passionately on gum that kept her jaws firm and circling.

Suddenly the chorus rose shriller. Flegg had veered slightly towards the safer staircase. His eyes had naturally questioned this along with the rest of the gasometer, and almost unconsciously his footsteps had veered in the direction of his eyes; then this instinct had emerged into full consciousness—perhaps he could use the staircase, no one had actually instanced the Jacob's ladder, there might yet be a chance? But the quick eyes behind him had seen, and immediately the chorus rose, "No you don't!" "Not up those sissy stairs!" Flegg switched his course by only the fraction that turned him again to the perpendicular ladder. "Who's talking about stairs?" he shouted back.

Behind him they still kept up a din, still kept him up to pitch, worrying at him viciously. "Look at him, he doesn't know which way to go—he's like a ruddy duck's uncle without an aunt."

So that Flegg realized finally that there was no alternative. He had to climb the gasometer by the vertical ladder. And as soon as this was finally settled, the doubt cleared from his mind. He braced his shoulders and suddenly found himself really making light of the job. After all, he thought, it isn't so high? Why should I worry? Hundreds of men climb such ladders each day, no one falls, the ladders are clamped as safe as houses! He began to smile within himself at his earlier perturbations. Added to this, the girl now ran up to him and handed him her handkerchief. As her black eyes frowned a smile at him, he saw that her expression no longer held its vicious laughing scorn, but now instead had grown softer, with a look of real encouragement and even admiration. "Here's your flag," she said. And then she even added, "Tell you what—you don't really have to go! I'll believe you!" But this came too late. Flegg had accepted the climb, it was fact, and already he felt something of an exhilarating glow of glory. He took the handkerchief, blew the girl a dramatic kiss, and started up the lowest rungs of the ladder at a run.

This painter's ladder was placed at a comfortable slant. But nevertheless Flegg had only climbed some ten feet—what might have corresponded to the top of a first-floor window—when he began to slow up, he stopped running and gripped harder at the rungs above and placed his feet more firmly on the unseen bars below. Although he had not yet measured his distance from the ground, somehow he sensed distinctly that he was already unnaturally high, with nothing but air and a precarious skeleton of wooden bars between him and the receding ground. He felt independent of solid support; yet, according to his eyes, which stared straight forward at the iron sheeting beyond, he might have been still standing on the lowest rungs by the ground. The sensation of height infected him strongly, it had become an urgent necessity to maintain a balance, each muscle of his body became unnaturally alert. This was not an unpleasant feeling, he almost enjoyed a new athletic command of every precarious movement. He climbed then methodically until he reached the ladderhead and the first of the perpendicular iron rungs.

Here for a moment Flegg had paused. He had rested his knees up against the last three steps of the safely-slanting wooden ladder, he had grasped the two side supports of the rusted iron that led so straightly upwards. His knees then clung to the motherly wood, his hands felt the iron cold and gritty. The rust powdered off and smeared him with its red dust; one large scrap flaked off and fell on to his face as he looked upwards. He wanted to brush this away from his eye, but the impulse was, to his surprise, much less powerful than the vice-like will that clutched his hands to the iron support. His hand remained firmly gripping the iron, he had to shake off the rust-flake with a jerk of his head. Even then this sharp movement nearly unbalanced him, and his stomach gulped coldly with sudden shock. He settled his knees more firmly against the wood, and though he forced himself to laugh at this sudden fear, so that in some measure his poise did really return, nevertheless he did not alter the awkward knock-kneed position of his legs patently clinging for safety. With all this he had scarcely paused. Now he pulled at the stanchions of the iron ladder, they were as firm as if they had been driven into rock.

He looked up, following the dizzying rise of the rungs to the skyline. From this angle flat against the iron sheeting, the gasometer appeared higher than before. The blue sky seemed to descend and almost touch it. The redness of the rust dissolved into a deepening grey shadow, the distant curved summit loomed over black and high. Although it was immensely stable, as seen in rounded perspective from a few yards away, there against the side it appeared top heavy, so that this huge segment of sheet iron seemed to have lost the support of its invisible complement behind, the support that was now unseen and therefore unfelt, and Flegg imagined despite himself that the entire erection had become unsteady, that quite possibly the gasometer might suddenly blow over like a gigantic top-heavy sail. He lowered his eyes quickly and concentrated on the hands before him. He began to climb.

From beneath there still rose a few cries from the boys. But the girl had stopped shouting—probably she was following Flegg's every step with admiring eyes. He imagined again her frown and her peculiarly pouting mouth, and from this image drew new strength with which he clutched the rungs more eagerly. But now he noticed that the cries had begun to ring with an unpleasant new echo, as though they were already far off. And Flegg could not so easily distinguish their words. Even at this height he seemed to have penetrated into a distinct stratum of separate air, for it was certainly cooler, and for the first time that day he felt the light fanning of a wind. He looked down. His friends appeared shockingly small. Their bodies had disappeared and he saw only their upturned faces. He wanted to wave, to demonstrate in some way a carefree attitude; but then instantly he felt frustrated as his hands refused to unlock their grip. He turned to the rungs again with the smile dying on his lips.

He swallowed uneasily and continued to tread slowly upwards, hand after hand, foot after foot. He had climbed ten rungs of the iron ladder when his hands first began to feel moist, when suddenly, as though a catastrophe had overtaken him not gradually but in one overpowering second, he realized that he was afraid; incontrovertibly. He could cover it no longer, he admitted it all over his body. His hands gripped with pitiable eagerness, they were now alert to a point of shivering, as though the nerves inside them had been forced taut for so long that now they had burst beyond their strained tegument; his feet no longer trod firmly on the rungs beneath, but first stepped for their place timorously, then glued themselves to the iron. In this way his body lost much of its poise; these nerves and muscles in his two legs and two arms seemed to work independently, no longer integrated with the rhythm of his body, but moving with the dangerous unwilled jerk of crippled limbs.

His body hung slack away from the ladder, with nothing beneath it but a thirty foot drop to the ground; only his hands and feet were fed with the security of an attachment, most of him lay off the ladder, hanging in space; his arms revolted at the strain of their unfamiliar angle, as though they were flies' feet denying all natural laws. For the first time, as the fear took hold of him, he felt that what he had attempted was impossible. He could never achieve the top. If at this height of only thirty feet, as it were three storeys of a building, he felt afraid—what would he feel at sixty feet? Yet . . . he trod heavily up. He was afraid, but not desperate. He dreaded each step, yet forced himself to believe that at some time it would be over, it could not take long.

A memory crossed his mind. It occurred to him vividly, then flashed away, for his eyes and mind were continually concentrated on the rusted iron bars and the white knuckles of his hands. But for an instant he remembered waking up long ago in the nursery and seeing that the windows were light, as if they reflected a coldness of moonlight. Only they were not so much lit by light as by a sensation of space. The windows seemed to echo with space. He had crawled out of bed and climbed on to a chair that stood beneath the window. It was as he had thought. Outside there was space, nothing else, a limitless area of space; yet this was not unnatural, for soon his logical eyes had supplied for what had at first appeared an impossible infinity the later image of a perfectly reasonable flood. A vast plain of still water continued as far as his eyes could see. The tennis courts and the houses beyond had disappeared; they were quite submerged, flat motionless water

135

spread out immeasurably to the distant arced horizon all around. It lapped silently at the sides of the house, and in the light of an unseen moon winked and washed darkly, concealing great beasts of mystery beneath its black calm surface. This water attracted him, he wished to jump into it from the window and immerse himself in it and allow his head to sink slowly under. However he was perched up too high. He felt, alone at the window, infinitely high, so that the flood seemed to lie in miniature at a great distance below, as later in life when he was ill he had seen the objects of his bedroom grow small and infinitely remote in the fevered reflection behind his eyes. Isolated at the little window he had been frightened by the emptiness surrounding him, only the sky and the water and the marooned stone wall of the house; he had been terrified yet drawn down by dread and desire.

Then a battleship had sailed by. He had woken up, saved by the appearance of the battleship. And now on the ladder he had a sudden hope that something as large and stable would intervene again to help him.

But ten rungs farther up he began to sweat more violently than ever. His hands streamed with wet rust, the flesh inside his thighs blenched. Another flake of rust fell on his forehead; this time it stuck in the wetness. He felt physically exhausted. Fear was draining his strength, and the precarious position of his body demanded an awkward physical effort. From his outstretched arms suspended most of the weight of his body. Each stressed muscle ached. His body weighed more heavily at each step upwards, it sagged beneath his arms like a leaden sack. His legs no longer provided their adequate support; it seemed as though they needed every pull of their muscle to force themselves, as independent limbs, close to the ladder. The wind blew faster. It dragged now at his coat, it blew its space about him, it echoed silently a lonely spaciousness. "Don't look down," the blood whispered in his temples, "Don't look down, for God's sake, DON'T LOOK DOWN."

Three-quarters up the gasometer, and fifty feet from the

ground, Flegg grew desperate. Every other consideration suddenly left him. He wanted only to reach the ground as quickly as possible, only that. Nothing else mattered. He stopped climbing and clung to the ladder panting. Very slowly, lowering his eyes carefully so that he could raise them instantly if he saw too much, he looked down a rung, and another, past his armpit, past his waist—and focused them on the ground beneath. He looked quickly up again.

He pressed himself to the ladder. Tears started in his eyes. For a moment they reeled red with giddiness. He closed them, shutting out everything. Then instantly opened them, afraid that something might happen. He must watch his hands, watch the bars, watch the rusted iron sheeting itself; no movement should escape him; the struts might come creaking loose, the whole edifice might sway over; although a fading reason told him that the gasometer had remained firm for years and was still as steady as a cliff, his horrified senses suspected that this was the one moment in the building's life when a wind would blow that was too strong for it, some defective strut would snap, the whole edifice would heel over and go crashing to the ground. This image became so clear that he could see the sheets of iron buckling and folding like cloth as the huge weight sank to the earth.

The ground had receded horribly, the drop now appeared terrifying, out of all proportion to this height he had reached. From the ground such a height would have appeared unnoteworthy. But now looking down the distance seemed to have doubled. Each object familiar to his everyday eyes—his friends, the lamp-posts, a brick wall, the kerb, a drain—all these had grown infinitely small. His senses demanded that these objects should be of a certain accustomed size. Alternatively, the world of chimneys and attic windows and roof-coping would grow unpleasantly giant as his pavement-bred eyes approached. Even now the iron sheeting that stretched to either side and above and below seemed to have grown, he was lost among such huge smooth dimensions, grown smaller himself and clinging now like a child lost on some monstrous desert of red dust.

These unfamiliarities shocked his nerves more than the danger of falling. The sense of isolation was overpowering. All things were suddenly alien. Yet exposed on the iron spaces, with the unending winds blowing aerially round him, among such free things—he felt shut in! Trembling and panting so that he stifled himself with the shortness of his own breath, he took the first step downwards. . . .

A commotion began below. A confusion of cries came drifting up to him. Above all he could hear the single voice of the girl who had so far kept quiet. She was screaming high, a shrill scream that rose in the air incisively like a gull's shriek. "Put it back, put it back, put it back!" the scream seemed to say. So that Flegg, thinking that these cries were to warn him of some new danger apparent only from the ground—Flegg gripped himself into the ladder and looked down again. He glanced down only for a fractional second—but in that time saw enough. He saw that the quiet girl was screaming and pointing to the base of the iron ladder. He saw the others crowding round her, gesticulating. He saw that she really had been crying, "Put it back!" And he realized now what the words meant—someone had removed the painter's ladder.

It lay clearly on the ground, outlined white like a child's drawing of a ladder. The boys must have seen his first step downwards, and then, from fun or from spite they had removed his only means of retreat. He remembered that from the base of the iron ladder to the ground the drop fell twenty feet. He considered quickly descending and appealing from the bottom of the ladder; but foresaw that for precious minutes they would jeer and argue, refusing to replace the ladder, and he felt then that he could never risk these minutes, unnerved, with his strength failing. Besides, he had already noticed that the whole group of them were wandering off. The boys were driving the quiet girl away, now more concerned with her than with Flegg. The quiet girl's sense of guilt had been brought to a head by the removal of the ladder. Now she was hysterically terrified. She was yelling to them to put the ladder back. She—only she, the passive one—sensed the terror that awaited them all. But her screams defeated their own purpose. They had altogether distracted the attention of the others; now it was fun to provoke more screams, to encourage this new distraction—and they forgot about Flegg far up and beyond them. They were wandering away. They were abandoning him, casually unconcerned that he was alone and helpless up in his wide prison of rust. His heart cried out for them to stay. He forgot their scorn in new and terrible torments of self-pity. An uneasy feeling lumped his throat, his eyes smarted with dry tears.

But they were wandering away. There was no retreat. They did not even know he was in difficulties. So Flegg had no option but to climb higher. Desperately he tried to shake off his fear, he actually shook his head. Then he stared hard at the rungs immediately facing his eyes, and tried to imagine that he was not high up at all. He lifted himself tentatively by one rung, then by another, and in this way dragged himself higher and higher . . . until he must have been some ten rungs from the top, over the fifth storey of a house, with now perhaps only one more storey to climb. He imagined that he might then be approaching the summit platform, and to measure this last distance he looked up.

He looked up and heaved. He felt for the first time panicked beyond desperation, wildly violently loose. He almost let go. His senses screamed to let go, yet his hands refused to open. He was stretched on a rack made by these hands that would not unlock their grip and by the panic desire to drop. The nerves left his hands, so that they might have been dried bones of fingers gripped round the rungs, hooks of bone fixed perhaps strongly enough to cling on, or perhaps ready at some moment of pressure to uncurl their vertebrae and straighten to a drop. His insteps pricked with cold cramp. The sweat sickened him. His loins seemed to empty themselves. His trousers ran wet. He shivered, grew giddy, and flung himself froglike on to the ladder.

The sight of the top of the gasometer had proved endemically more frightful than the appearance of the drop beneath. There lay about it a sense not of material danger, not of the risk of falling, but of something removed and unhuman—a sense of appalling isolation. It echoed its elemental iron aloofness, a wind blew round it that had never known the warmth of flesh nor the softness of green fibres. Its blind eyes were raised above the world. It might have been the eyeless iron vizor of an ancient god. It touched against the sky, having risen in awful perpendicular to this isolation, solitary as the grey gannet cliffs that mark the end of the northern world. It was immeasurably old, outside the connotation of time; it was nothing human, only washed by the high weather, echoing with wind, visited never, and silently alone.

And in this summit Flegg measured clearly the full distance of his climb. This close skyline emphasized the whirling space beneath him. He clearly saw a man fall through this space, spread-eagling to smash with the sickening force of a locomotive on the stone beneath. The man turned slowly in the air, yet his thoughts raced faster than he fell.

Flegg, clutching his body close to the rust, made small weeping sounds through his mouth. Shivering, shuddering, he began to tread up again, working his knees and elbows outwards like a frog, so that his stomach could feel the firm rungs. Were they firm? His ears filled with a hot roaring, he hurried himself, he began to scramble up, wrenching at his last strength, whispering urgent meaningless words to himself like the swift whispers that close in on a nightmare. A huge weight pulled at him, dragging him to drop. He climbed higher. He reached the top rung—and found his face staring still at a wall of red rust. He looked, wild with terror. It was the top rung! The ladder had ended! Yet—no platform . . . the real top rungs were missing . . . the platform jutted five impassable feet above ... Flegg stared dumbly, circling his head like a lost animal ... then he jammed his legs in the lower rungs and his arms past the elbows to the armpits in through the top rungs and there he hung shivering and past knowing what more he could ever do. ...

Fear

H. E. BATES

ON the horizon three separate thunderstorms talked
darkly to each other.

The hut where little Richard and his grandfather had taken
shelter was already green with darkness, its air stifling and
warm, and the trees that surrounded it purple and heavy
with whispers. When the boy heard sounds coming from the
wood he would turn upwards a pair of great eyes, faint-yellow
with fear, and ask in an awed voice:

"What's the matter, Grandfather? What makes it dark?"

At one time the man would scratch his beard and say nothing, at another grunt and say, "Don't you worry yourself,"
and at another, "You ain't frightened are you? You're too big
a boy to be frightened. You sit still. You'll wear your breeches
out."

But the child would never cease to cast his great swollen
eyes about the hut, fidget on trembling haunches and show
that he was afraid of the dark and oppressive silence and the
growls of thunder which dropped into it, reminding him
dreadfully of the voices of cows and dogs. So he saw nothing
tiresome in repeating:

"What's the matter, Grandfather? What makes it dark?"

Each time he said this it seemed that there was less to be
seen in the hut, and not much outside either, where the three
thunderstorms grew angrier and angrier with each other, and
that in the wood the trees were beginning to open their arms
in readiness to catch the approaching rain. And when this did

not come the old man wetted his soft lips, told the boy he would sing him something and began a ballad.

Beyond the first note or two, however, the boy did not listen, and in a few moments the thin tune gave up its exploration of the stagnant air, and the man said again:

"You sit still. There's nothing to hurt."

"What's it dark for then?" persisted the boy.

"It's going to rain."

He could not understand this.

"Yesterday it rained and the sun shone," he said. "Why doesn't the sun shine now?"

"The sun ain't here."

"Where's it gone?" he asked.

"Don't you worry."

And again it thundered. The boy could scarcely see his grandfather, and when all was silent he went to the door and peered out. Coming back he caught a smell like bad fish from the dirty floor of the hut, wondering why it smelt like that. Before long he began to cry.

"What makes the sky green?" he asked.

"It ain't green!" his grandfather declared.

"It is," he persisted, blubbering. "It's green like Nancy's hat. What makes it green?"

"It's going to rain," was the answer. "That's all. You be quiet."

He wept again in reply. As he looked up through the window the film of his tears made it seem as if the black sky was pushing the trees down on the hut and that before very long would crush it and bury him. "I want to go home," he whispered, but the man did not answer, and for a long while there was a sultry silence. The boy felt himself sweating. He could not see his grandfather and wanted to find him desperately but dare not move an inch. And as he stood there it began to rain, at first desultorily, then thickly and with a great hissing sound.

"Grandfather! Grandfather!" He wept and ran at last

between the man's dark knees. "Grandfather!" he whimpered.

There were sleepy grunts in reply.

"Wake up!" the little one whispered. "It's raining. I want to go home. Wake up!"

When the old man aroused himself it was to hear immense shaking rolls of thunder, the boy's voice in tears, and the rain throwing itself against the window in a sort of grey passion.

"I want to go home!" the boy cried. "It's night. Mamma'll have gone to bed."

"You be quiet," comforted the man. "It ain't night."

"Then what time is it?"

Like a white eye a watch came out in the gloom, a bluish match-flame spurted over it, and for a minute the boy was unafraid, gazed awfully at the leaf-shaped light, its reflections on his grandfather's face, the watch and the roof of the hut and forgot the storm and his fear.

"It's only eight o'clock," his grandfather growled without ill-will. "You sit quiet."

But at that moment the flame seemed to get swallowed by the darkness, and as if by some malicious miracle next moment appear again in a frenzied light that gave the sky a yellow wound which in turn spilt yellow blood on the wood and the dark floor of the hut. There came thunder, as if a great beast sat roaring on the roof. The hot peaceable air seemed to cry out like a sensitive child, the trees were distressed, the great confusion made the boy's head thick and hot with terror.

He buried his head in the friendly cavern between the man's thighs and there groaned and wept in darkness.

And as the thunder and lightning made their terrifying duet above his head, he tried to think of his home, his mother's cool face, the windows where there were blinds and harmless moths, but he managed it all vaguely and felt that what prevented him was the storm, which was something black and cunning and old, and against which he had no chance. Only if he remained half-eaten up by the shadows and were mistaken for a dog or sack might he perhaps escape. And so he crouched there, very still, trying not to listen, but hearing everything in a greater tumult than ever, and knew that the storm went on without heeding his fear.

Nearly an hour passed: often the boy wanted to cry out, but felt as if choked by fear and darkness and kept silent. His knees grew cold, one leg fell into a tingling sleep, only his head was warm and throbbed madly like an old clock. Once there was a smell of burning from the wood, but it passed, and the boy forgot it in wondering if animals were terrified as he was, and where all the birds had gone and why they were silent. Then by some lucky chance he caught the silvery ticks of his grandfather's watch and was comforted.

So it grew quiet and a clear darkness came. The boy got up and opened his eyes. The rain no longer growled, and soon the thunder passed off. Outside the cobwebs hung like ropes of leaden beads and the ground was covered with great shadow-printed pools over which the man lifted the boy. From the edge of the wood were visible the blue storms, retreated far off in a mist, and a star or two in the course they had used.

"There's the cuckoo!" the man said.

It was true, and as the boy listened he forgot the last of his fear. When he tried to walk he discovered his legs were stiff, and that when he set it down one foot tingled as if a thousand pins had been pressed into it, and he laughed.

For diversion the man told old stories, which the child heard vaguely, and when that grew stale, held the boy's forefinger in his own rugged palm and counted the stars.

"Fifty-one, fifty-two."

And though one or twice lightning came there was no thunder, and because of the increasing stars it seemed to the boy that the storm had lost all terror for him, that perhaps he had been asleep when the most terrible flashes came, and that soon the village would come and from then onwards no fear.

"I'm not frightened, Grandfather," he said a dozen times.

Then, as it struck nine o'clock and the boy listened to the notes roaming about the dark fields, he saw a star shoot.

145

"A star fell down! A star fell down!" he immediately cried. "Oh! it fell like——"

He was seized with joy, punched the man's legs, jumped into a pool and cried again:

"A star fell down!"

But his grandfather said nothing.

In the superstition that a falling star means death the man did not wholly believe, but for some reason he could not help recalling it suddenly. As he went down the hill his mind became restive, and he thought of his wife, of her death, then of his own age, his stale limbs and the possibility of his dying. And gradually he felt he was doomed to die soon and he began to sweat, as the boy had done, and was oppressed by the idea of something terrible and black waiting in readiness to crush the life from him, and that against it all he had no chance. He felt weak and depressed in body and soul.

One or two birds began to chirp and the boy heard them, but like the man he thought only of the star. He remembered he must ask why in the hut there was a smell of fish, if animals were afraid, and where birds hid during the storm, but looking up into his grandfather's face saw it serious with fearful shadows and gleams and he dared only say:

"Did you see the star fall?"

There was no reply. As they walked down the hill the man, becoming more and more stricken by the fear of death, could not hold himself still. But the boy would only laugh, and while watching for other stars to shoot, wonder with perplexity why his grandfather looked stern and miserable, hurried along as if it were going to rain again, and never spoke to him.

Thoughts and Questions to guide reading

These are not intended to be academic tasks but to assist deeper perception about the stories. They can of course be ignored.

Key of the Cabinet

1. This story may well be set in a part of the country as remote from your own as it is also distant in time. Find details which make the world of the key-strikers as real to you as your own.

2. Both Bill and Ernie try to get a free go from fortunate possessors of keys and explosives. Compare the wording of the refusals they get.

3. Superficially the boys appear rough (consider their speech and their footwear) but they both have gentle and kindly qualities. Find examples of these.

4. Why was Ernie's mother so grateful to him? How did she show her gratitude?

5. Every line of the story deserves separate consideration. Consider the special interest of these lines:
   (a) Ernie was too bony to be tempting (*page* 11).
   (b) My dad's Chippendale Chinese cabinet (*page* 12).
   (c) Then doors shot open all over the street, and dogs barked, and all the lads came running around (*page* 13).
   (d) Ee, I thought it was God had done it (*page* 15).
   (e) Sir King, behold an arm clothed in white samite, mystic wonderful (*page* 16).

147

The Harvesting

1. See how many references you can find to the heat.

2. Then observe how many of these references show that Grooby is feeling the heat more than anybody else.

3. Why is he enduring all this discomfort? Is he the hero that he thinks himself on page 20? He says that he wants to "enjoy the harvest"!

4. What hints does Hughes give us as to the cause of Grooby's poor state of health? His poor condition has made him sensitive not only to the heat but also to noise. Find evidence of this.

5. Grooby has three attacks. The account of his experience during the second attack (partly caused by his first shot at the hare) is rather confusing. This confusion is intentional. Can you see why?

6. In the last paragraph Grooby has a third attack. Perhaps it is a final, fatal attack; we are not told. But the author is directing us to compare Grooby with the hare at this moment. In what ways are their experiences similar?

7. The author has directed our sympathies, making us dislike Grooby from the beginning. (Even his name is unpleasant.) Look for details which lead us to dislike Grooby and sympathize with the hare. Contrast his opinion of his shooting with his performance.

8. The story is full of significant touches. Why are the following particularly significant?
    (*a*) The best sport of all . . . usually comes in the last ten minutes (*page* 18).
    (*b*) The spluttering reports, the dense machine-gun bursts from the tractor (*page* 19).
    (*c*) Grooby held his gun in the crook of his left arm, like a baby, fondling the chased side-plates and trigger-guard (*page* 20).

    (*d*) Trying to recognize the strangely shorn hill-side (*page* 22).

    (*e*) He adopted his brusquest managerial air, putting the farmer and this gang of impudent, anonymous colliers' faces back into place (*page* 25).

    (*f*) Every clump of wheat had ears (*page* 26).

    (*g*) The delicate lines of its thin face (*page* 26).

The Barber's Trade Union

1. The opening paragraph is very important. It first looks forward to Chandu's achievements. (What actions earned Chandu his right to a place in history?) It also suggests that Chandu achieved more than he knew he was achieving. What was this achievement which Anand regards as of historical importance?

2. The story presents us with a way of life in a land remote from our experience. See how many details you can find of the kind which make the background vivid to you.

3. Chandu was of a lower caste than Anand. Why does Anand admire Chandu so much? Distinguish between things which Anand admired because he was still a schoolboy and qualities which really make Chandu superior.

4. Why do you think this sentence is important in revealing Anand's attitude to the caste system of India? "But whatever innate ideas I had inherited from my forefathers, I certainly had not inherited any sense of superiority" (*page* 29).

5. What do you think was the reason for the "suffering and humiliations" which Chandu's mother had endured through sixty years? (*page* 33).

6. Do not allow yourself to be baffled by strange words. The meaning of most of them can be deduced from the context.

> (a) What is the Subedar likely to be if he bequeathed Chandu his worn-out *khaki* shorts? (*page* 29).
>
> (b) 'Chaprasis' is harder, but you can get near enough to the meaning from its position in the list "the Sahibs and the lawyers, the chaprasis and the policemen (of) the District Court" (*page* 30).

7. Don't overlook the significance of "steal" (*page* 29). It gives a special meaning to "where he had to wait for the journey home at the back of Lalla Hukam Chand's phaeton" (*page* 30).

8. Don't miss the humour of pages 30–31: what the missionary teacher looked like to the Indians.

9. What is the contrast that the phrase "emoluments of his professional skill" is being used to highlight? (*page* 30).

10. Bijay Chand was serious when he said "... we will have to treat the whole house with the sacred cow-dung to purify it." Why does this seem funny to us? Do you think Anand intends us to laugh at this? (*page* 31).

Sredni Vashtar

1. Mrs De Ropp was Conradin's cousin and guardian, not his mother. She *appeared* to be concerned for his health and well-being. What did she not give him? What was Conradin's attitude to her?

2. Note what is unusual about the boy himself.

3. "The few fruit-trees that it contained were set jealously apart from his plucking." Why was Conradin not allowed to pick the fruit? (*page* 40).

4. Conradin lavished affection on the Houdan hen. Consider this fact in relation to your answer to Question 1. What did he feel for the polecat-ferret? (Consider the name of the ferret and what it suggests, and notice what the tool-shed was used for.)

5. "Do one thing for me, Sredni Vashtar." Why does the boy not say exactly what that thing is? (*page 42*).

6. On *page* 41 the author refers to "her short-sighted eyes". What is the importance of this fact later?

7. What view do the servants have of Conradin? What do they expect the boy's reaction to be when they tell him what has happened to his guardian? How does he show his real feelings in the last paragraph?

8. Does the victim deserve her fate, do you think? Examine closely your own response to this story: do you "enjoy" it?

A Story

1. Perhaps it is not a story, but it is full of enjoyment for the reader because the boy who observed the events and the writer who recorded them enjoyed them: "My uncle ... used to fill every inch of the hot little house like an old buffalo squeezed into an airing cupboard" (*page 45*).

2. Much of the humour comes from exaggeration; exaggeration never intended to deceive us: "the loud check meadow of his waistcoat was littered, as though after a picnic, with cigarette ends, peelings, cabbage-stalks, birds' bones, gravy; and the forest-fire of his hair crackled. . . ." (*page 45*).

3. All one can do with Dylan Thomas at his best is quote and wish a typewriter could print with a Welsh accent:
   "Do you think I'*m* going to drink the outing funds, like Bob the Fiddle did?" said Mr Franklyn.
   "You *might*," said my uncle slowly. . . .
   My uncle put on his spectacles ... took Mr Franklyn's list of names, removed the spectacles so that he could read, and then ticked the names off one by one. "Enoch Davies. Aye. He's good with his fists. . . ." (*page 47*).

Remember this fact when you read the public-house conversation in the Hermit's Nest:

"I played for Aberavon in 1898," said a stranger to Enoch Davies.

"Liar," said Enoch Davies.

"I can show you photos," said the stranger.

"Forged," said Enoch Davies.

"And I'll show you my cap at home."

"Stolen."

"I got friends to prove it," the stranger said in a fury.

"Bribed," said Enoch Davies (*page 53*).

A Shoni-Onion Breton man, with a beret and a necklace of onions, bicycled down the road and stopped at the door.

"Quelle un grand matin, monsieur," I said.

"There's French, boy bach!" he said (*page 51*).

And, when a policeman entered the Druid's Tap by the back door, and found them all choral with beer, "Sssh!" said Noah Bowen, "the pub is shut" (*page 52*).

"Who goes there?" called out Will Sentry to the flying moon.

4. *The Key of the Cabinet* is chiefly concerned with a "child's-eye view" of the child's world: *A Story* also has a boy as the observer and story-teller, but he is observing an adult world. It is an impression of adults out celebrating. Compare the two boys'-eye views; how do they differ? How do adults come out of each of these stories— well? badly? or perhaps, humanly? This one has a certain air of fantasy about it. Single out some of the moments which seem to have this feeling about them.

Thithyphuth, or my Uncle's Waiter

1. Consider the difference between the waiter and the uncle —they both have the same speech defect, and yet they are different. In what way? (Consider, for example, the last words of the uncle. Why are these particularly amusing? Examine also the many words the author uses to point the contrast earlier in the story.)

2. How did the uncle's speech defect nearly lead to a brawl?

3. The quarrel is laughable and absurd—what sort of thing takes place to make it so?

4. The upshot is far from absurd, however. Why is this? How does the author prevent the pair from seeming simply silly?

5. How do they become friends? What contribution did the author (as a boy) make to bring about this friendship? What do the waiter sitting down at the table and the bringing of the brandies signify?

6. Find out about the legend of Sisyphus. How does it relate to the experience of the waiter and the uncle apart from the former having had to pronounce it at school?

7. You will be able to see readily and to discuss the relevance of this story to other kinds of handicapped people, but is it only applicable to such people? What reference does it have to all of us?

Casting the Runes

To enjoy a M. R. James ghost story properly one must be alert to miss no clues:

1. What significance does this statement have: ". . . he was coming out of the British Museum gate as I drove past"? (*page* 70).

2. Why did Karswell entertain the village children with a magic-lantern?

3. After reading the notice on the window the tram conductor said, "Well that's a cure, ain't it?" (*page* 75). Compare the Harrington "advert" with the advertisement which Dunning had been reading before.

4. What significance do you attach to these references?
    (*a*) It seemed unnaturally rough and hot (*page* 78).
    (*b*) a gust of warm, or even hot air played for an instant round his shins (*page* 80).
    (*c*) both men noticed that the carriage seemed to darken about them and to grow warmer (*page* 90).

5. Karswell passed the runes he had cast both to John Harrington and to Dunning; what were the means he used in each case?

6. What significance do you attach to this passage on *page* 84?
    "Well," I said, "you can't give it back now."
    He said nothing for a minute: then rather crossly, "No, I can't; but why you should keep on saying so I don't know."

7. What was significant about the day of Karswell's death, July 23?

8. Why did Harrington buy a set of Bewick at the Karswell sale?

The Enemy

1. When you have finished the story re-read the first sentence and the last. What change has taken place in the boy's attitude to his mother?

2. When do you first realize that his mother cares for the boy?

154

3. "In fact, Cunupia and Tableland are the two parts of Trinidad where murders occur often enough to ensure quick promotion for the policemen stationed there" (*page 93*).

   Why is the promotion quick for them there?

4. Why did the boy's mother leave the father?

5. When you first read "I was travelling ... the chickens began squawking", you think he is travelling on a bus. What makes you realize that this is just an impression he has as he regains consciousness? (*page 102*).

The Burglars

The children in *The Golden Age*, from which this story is taken, were separated from their parents, who lived abroad, and the adults who acted as foster-parents remained somewhat aloof and remote. So the children tended to lead independent lives and to refer to their guardians as the Olympians.

The children are young—Edward, the eldest, is probably no more than ten—and the reader gets amusement from their misunderstanding of the motives and the actions of their elders. The narrator, Kenneth, is younger than Edward but although he took part in the escapade as a nine-year-old he relates the story as an adult. Thus we get two kinds of comment from Kenneth: it is the child Kenneth who asks, "What's spooning?" and the adult Kenneth who ruminates thus: "Silence ensued, both our minds being busy with the new situation thus presented: mine, in wonderment at this flaw that so often declared itself in enviable natures of fullest endowment—in a grown-up man and a good cricketer, for instance, even as this curate...." But even so it is the language that is adult; the thought is the child's (*page 103*).

1. What does the author want to convey about the boy's idea of Aunt Maria by the remark in brackets that she "must have seen some five-and-twenty summers"? (*page 103*).

2. What kind of book do you suppose the "rotten book" was that Bobby Ferris had quoted from to his sister's boyfriend? (*page* 105).

3. Why did his yarn not convince the boyfriend? Examine the choice of the boy's words and manner of expression.

4. Where does a style like that of "the rotten book" recur later in the story?

5. Why did the teller of the story always have to dodge the curate subsequently?

Holding Her Down

1. To enjoy this story you must master the jargon used by the tramp, travelling on the railway without a ticket (or as London says "a hobo on the bum"). These terms he either defines or makes clear indirectly:

   (*a*) A shack (*page* 110).
   (*b*) A blind (*page* 113).
   (*c*) Gone underneath, on the rods (*page* 110).
   (*d*) Decking her (*page* 118).

2. "This dropping out was the measure of their skill and nerve in boarding a train" (*page* 114). How did London show his superiority to the other hoboes? He exults in his superiority: "And furthermore, was I not a tramp-royal? Were not these other tramps mere dubs and 'gay-cats' and amateurs alongside of me?" (*page* 115).

3. But he was not only better than the tramps, he was better than the shacks: "Out ahead, in the darkness—so far ahead that the shack riding out the blind must perforce get off before it reaches me—I get on" (*page* 115).

4. "I have taught them that they cannot guard the train from me. They must do something else" (*page* 122). What do they do?

5. The climax of this story comes when at last they "ditch" him (*page* 124). How does he outwit the train's guards then?

6. Finally he sleeps peacefully among the coal of a freighter which has waited for the overland express to go ahead of it on the single track. How does he outwit the conductor?

7. Once you have reached the end you realize the importance of what London said in his opening paragraph: "A good hobo, with youth and agility, can hold a train down despite all the efforts of the train-crew to 'ditch' him." What evidence have you found of this youthful agility and of his delight in his skill? Note how the engineer pays tribute to London's skill and how pleased he is to find it recognized: " 'You son-of-a-gun,' is what he says. It is a high compliment, and I thrill as a schoolboy thrills on receiving a reward of merit" (*pages* 121–122).

The Vertical Ladder

1. What made Flegg climb the gasometer?

2. How does the nature of the gasometer change for the boy as he climbs? How does the boy's view of it alter as the story progresses?

3. What was the effect of the removal of the lower ladder?

4. Flegg "switched his course". To where? Why? (*page* 131).

5. If he did not see the importance of such phrases as "an hysterical accumulation of spite" and "underlying unpleasantness" a reader might dismiss the "dare" as little more than a joke. What more does the writer suggest there is to it? (*page* 129).

6. "A memory crossed his mind . . ." (*page* 135). This paragraph is worth considering very closely: notice that Sansom in describing the boy's childhood memory in two

different places here says that he "remembered waking up" and that he "had woken up", *i.e.*, as if he woke up twice in succession. Do these mean the same thing then?

7. What is the significance of the battleship?

8. What does the author gain by leaving us in ignorance of Flegg's fate?

9. The story may lead you on to further discussion of such questions as the different causes of fear in yourself, how you cope with them, what you dread most—physical or other stress, and so on. Recall your childhood fears, for example. Have they all passed? Which remain with you, if any? What other fears have taken their place?

   The story also centres on pride and on what we call a "dare". This sort of thing too you can probably recall from childhood. Most "dares" are trivial: what major "dares" can you remember from your own life? Did you accept or ignore them? See if you can recollect the way you thought which led up to your acceptance or rejection of the challenge given to you.

   Do you think this sort of pride is something people grow out of—even after the "dares" of childhood are no longer part of their lives? How much does the opinion of others affect us in our actions?

Fear

1. At the beginning of the story why is the boy afraid?

2. Notice how the storm is made more terrifying by the suggestion that the elements and the natural surroundings are human: "On the horizon three separate thunderstorms *talked* darkly to each other." See how many other examples of this you can find.

3. At the beginning the author says "The hut ... was already green with darkness." Later the boy says, "What makes the sky green?"

"It ain't green!" his grandfather declared. Why do you think the boy was right?

4. At the end of the story the boy is happy. What has removed his fear? But the old man is unhappy. What has made him feel so?